Upping Your Ziggy

*How **David Bowie**
Faced His Childhood Demons
– and How **You** Can Face Yours*

Oliver James

KARNAC

First published in 2016 by
Karnac Books
118 Finchley Road
London NW3 5HT

British Library Cataloguing in Publication Data

A C.I.P. card for this book is available from the British Library

ISBN: 978–1–78220–490–9

Edited, designed, and produced by Communication Crafts

Printed in Great Britain by TJ International Ltd, Padstow, Cornwall

www.karnacbooks.com

Finding
Your Ziggy

To Gillon Aitken

CONTENTS

ACKNOWLEDGEMENTS

Many thanks to Nicholas Humphrey and Daniel Dennet for their and the journal's permission to use excerpts from their 1989 paper 'Speaking for Ourselves', *Raritan: A Quarterly Review*, Vol. 9, No. 1, pp. 68–98; reprinted courtesy of The MIT Press from *Brainchildren: Essays on Designing Minds*, by Daniel C. Dennett. Many thanks to Stephen Page and Emma Cheshire of Faber & Faber, and to the Larkin Estate, for their kind forbearance in providing me with permission to reproduce 'This Be The Verse' by Philip Larkin for the fourth time in one of my books.

I owe a debt to the book *Alias David Bowie* by Peter and Leni Gillman (1987), which provided much of the evidence regarding Bowie's childhood.

The many quotations of Bowie's words in the book are garnered from a great variety of sources, most of them BBC radio and television programmes. Since this is not primarily a psychobiography, to save space I have not cited the sources.

Thanks to my friends Paul and Anita Bamborough for the use of their house at a critical stage in the writing.

Special thanks to Oliver Rathbone for taking this book on. Karnac Books is possibly the only publisher who would consider it for publication. Oliver was open to a book that crosses quite a few genres while being ultimately grounded

Acknowledgements

in the tradition of the psychological analysis of public figures started by Sigmund Freud.

Thanks to Eric and Klara King for their painstaking work as editors.

Thanks to my children, Olive and Louis, for their continued forbearance in losing me to my computer when they would prefer me to be busy being their father.

Thanks, yet again, to my wife Clare, for having given me such helpful advice in ensuring that the content does not get too academic and gritty.

INTRODUCTION

Although David Bowie was one of the most famous and widely admired rock artists, few people know much about his family history. It is a remarkable story – as one might expect of such a remarkable man.

At its heart is the madness of three of his aunts on his mother's side of the family, and that of his half-brother, Terry. His fear that he was destined for insanity stalked him during the years of his greatest creations.

The nurture he received as a baby and small child left him vulnerable, but it also meant that from his mid-teens onwards, he was determined to become a rock star. That took many years, and the manner of its fulfilment makes for a powerful illustration of the therapeutic power of personas.

Before the invention and release of his album *The Rise And Fall Of Ziggy Stardust And The Spiders From Mars,* Bowie had achieved neither the acclaim nor the record sales he was convinced would one day be his. In acting the role of Ziggy Stardust, Bowie became a global star. But through this persona, he was also able to comfort himself and to address directly the fears created by his family history. So began a period in which he created several other selves that served the same purposes.

The heart of this book is not reached until Chapter 6 – the one about Ziggy Stardust. To be able to appreciate what I am suggesting there, you need to work your way through the previous chapters, which explain Bowie's family history and the scientific evidence revealing its significance.

At the simplest level, through creating Ziggy, Bowie fulfilled his ambition of rock stardom. But the Ziggy persona meant a great deal more than that to David Jones – which was Bowie's real name. You will see that Ziggy was a fiction invented by Bowie, who was, in his turn, another fiction. 'Rock 'N' Roll Suicide', the final song on the *Ziggy Stardust* album, has Bowie consoling Ziggy, thereby consoling Jones.

In the 1980s, Jones, now in his thirties, emerged a far more emotionally healthy man, one capable of eventually, after decades of sexual promiscuity and drug abuse, settling into a stable marriage in which he became a loving father. The key was the therapeutic use he had made of personas to develop authentic selves.

This aspect of Bowie's story might seem of little relevance to the 'ordinary' reader. But I believe it contains important clues to how most of us can enrich our personal and professional lives; and, indeed, Bowie was conscious of wanting to encourage us all to see that we have more potential than we often dare to think. In his period of greatest turmoil and yet also of creativity, bidding us to turn and face 'the stranger' – the one who seems strange to us, but also the stranger we see in the mirror – was a constant refrain. He wrestled with who he was and who he wanted to be and, in the process, urged us to do the same.

Working as a therapist, I have not met a single client who does not have several or numerous different selves – selves that I shall be calling 'personas'. My clients talk about the different parts of themselves, giving them names.

Edith, for example, was a high-achieving female civil servant who had, from a very young age, been colonised by her mother's unfulfilled ambitions. Having passed all her exams with top grades, she had flown up the civil service hierarchy. Although she had had love affairs, she had never married or had children. Now aged 48, she was, to her friends and colleagues, a charming, confident and impressive woman. But this was a mask; behind it was an angry person who was deeply frustrated because she had little idea of what she truly felt about almost anything. So completely had her needs and wishes been dictated by her mother that authentic self-determination was a mystery to her.

We began to talk about Good Edith as the smooth persona with which she dealt with everyone, including her friends. Since she never shared her true despair with any of them and had never done so throughout her life, her relationship with me was the first in which she revealed vulnerability and misery. As time went by, other Ediths emerged. There was Greedy Edith, who would gorge herself on ice cream, Mars bars and Thai food takeaways to the point of feeling sick. There was Madonna Edith, who had fantasies of dominating sexual conquests, a persona who would sometimes erupt on the Internet at weekends and late at night, engaging in virtual sex with strangers. There was Angry Edith, who imagined pulverising smug married friends who were living the life she sometimes wished for herself. And there was Baby Edith, who longed to be cuddled and cared for.

In our work we were gradually able to understand the history of each of these personas and their childhood origins, and this enabled Edith to be more conscious of the needs that lay behind them. As time went by, she began to see how her different moods were expressed through them and to consider how she might find more fruitful alternative personas. Eventually, she was able to relinquish Good Edith in her professional life, developing what she called Professional Edith, who was more assertive when that was required and softer at other times. Closer to her true feelings, she could express them better in that persona. In her personal life, she moved from the virtual to the actual, eventually finding a partner (as it happens, of her own sex) with whom she could playfully enjoy herself.

This is what I mean by Upping Your Ziggy: understanding the different parts of yourself better, identifying them and their origins, and then being much more self-conscious about which person you choose to be in different settings. For most of us, this does not require years of costly therapy.

It may be objected that, by definition, my clients are not typical of the general population. But the more I work as a therapist, the more convinced I become that this matter of personas is only a matter of degree. While some may have more personas than average, and while these personas may be less aware of each other, those are only extremes on a spectrum.

It is a commonplace that all of us are different people in different social roles – father, mother, worker, friend, lover. As T.S. Eliot elegantly expressed it, we must 'put on a face to meet the faces that we meet'. Our façades are meeting other façades when people gather together, but the extent to which each mask expresses the true person varies enormously.

Beyond my close family, I have known intimately dozens of people – friends and others. When you get to know someone well, you soon realise that they are not one person. For example, I have a friend who took up a hobby; within three years she was representing her country in international events. She dealt with her newcomer status to the game (which is largely dominated by men) by calling herself Gerald when playing it. In this guise, her self-doubts slipped away.

Introduction

Research in the last decade has eroded the bogus boundaries between madness and sanity which the psychiatric profession have sought to impose. Considerable numbers of us see visions and hear voices outside our heads. There are some striking examples of people who have these supposed symptoms of madness but who are conspicuously sane. If you watch the TED talk by Eleanor Longden*, a psychology lecturer and researcher at Liverpool University, you will see what I mean. I have met Eleanor on a number of occasions, and there is nothing odd about her.

In the TED talk she describes beginning to hear voices as an undergraduate – voices that became increasingly hostile as she fell apart under the stress created for her by the psychiatric system and the stigma that goes with 'mental illness' in our society. She came to realise that, although they were outside her, the voices were expressing feelings and traumas she had experienced as a child, but which had not been properly processed. She developed a dialogue with these voices and was, eventually, able to befriend them to such an extent that they helped her to get top marks in her university exams by telling her the answers – a form of cheating, as she jokes. Such voices were, she maintains, sane reactions to insane situations: she had suffered sexual abuse when young.

There are many ways for us to take charge of our personas – be it simply by self-reflection, the help of friends, creating novels or other artworks, or by therapy. How David Bowie was able to console David Jones through the persona of Ziggy Stardust is a particularly compelling example.

We can only speculate what was in Bowie's (or Jones's) mind when he planned his final album, ★ *(Blackstar)*. The mournful originality of its songs means that he lives on with us today, especially for those who have engaged with the discussion of the sorrow of dying. He remained filled with pretences until the end, realising himself through paradox.

Following Bowie's untimely death, many people have pointed out that his music alone was not his greatest gift to us – it was the idea that it's alright to be many different people.

ONE

Lyrical
– rather than actual –
madness

Many critics feel that David Bowie's greatest albums were produced between 1969 and 1974. Some of the work addressed the usual subjects of popular music like love and sex, but there was nothing commonplace about either his commentaries on them or his musical or dramatic presentation. Others of his songs travelled far from the beaten track of conventional pop or rock.

Speaking in 1975, Bowie explained what had driven the work of the previous five years:

'I was psychically damaged, I guess trying to get what I was understanding expressed in musical form.'

In 1976, he said:

'I hadn't been to an [psycho]analyst . . . my parents went, my brothers and sisters and my aunts and uncles and cousins, they did that. They ended up in a much worse state, so I stayed away. *I thought I'd write my problems out.*' [my emphasis]

In the activity of creating his work, he was trying to express his fears – a form of therapy, it could be said. In doing so, he was unwittingly starting from the premise that the wild and distressing thoughts and feelings that sometimes engulfed him were not just brain malfunctions, but had meaning.

Emil Kraepelin, a nineteenth-century German doctor, laid the faulty foundations upon which psychiatrists built their highly questionable edifice of psychiatric symptoms*. He claimed that these symptoms cannot be understood in terms of psychology: that they have no meaning and are, instead, a biological, largely genetic ailment, that is ultimately visible if the patient's diseased brain is examined. This model still prevails within psychiatry.

Textbooks divide mental illnesses into the discrete categories devised by Kraepelin. The diagnostic system reflects his basic assumptions about genetic causes and the need to explain to patients that they have a physical illness that does not differ in kind from tonsillitis. In 1978, the American psychiatrist Gerald Klerman updated Kraepelin, asserting that 'Psychiatry treats people who are sick and who require treatment for mental illness. . . . There is a boundary between the normal and sick. . . . There are discrete mental illnesses. . . . The focus of psychiatric physicians should be particularly on the biological aspects of mental illness*.'

But there is a stack of evidence that none of these claims stand up when scientifically tested and that Bowie was correct in treating his distress as meaningful.

First, the idea that there are distinct biological differences between people with psychoses and others is not proven. Reliable differences in patterns of brainwaves or damage to specific areas of the brain have yet to be found in people with psychoses. Indeed, this has now been explicitly acknowledged by the main scientist in charge of creating the latest version of the psychiatric bible, the *Diagnostic and Statistical Manual of Mental Disorders* (*DSM-5*)*. In the press release accompanying publication of the *DSM-5*, David Kupfer, who oversaw its creation, stated that 'We've been telling patients for several decades that we are waiting for biomarkers. *We're still waiting'* (my emphasis). While there are similarities in levels of chemicals and patterns of brainwaves between maltreated children and distressed adults, there are, as yet, no reliable, objective biological tests that can be used to identify who is mentally ill and who is not.

Second, considerably more of the population than expected have at least one symptom of madness, stretching its supposed boundary to breaking point*. For example, emotional stress makes seeing or hearing things much more likely, and so fully 13% of bereaved spouses have heard their dead partner's voice. Significant numbers of otherwise 'normal people' hear voices, and they may have conversations with them. Hallucinating sightings of familiar people is not uncommon. Delusions, such as that they have travelled in a UFO, are found in large swathes of the American population. Severely paranoid thoughts are surprisingly frequent.

Third, the notion that mental illnesses can be separated out from each other in discrete boxes is doubted by many distinguished figures in the field of psychology. Take manic-depressives – or people with bipolar disorder, as it is now termed. Their mania seems to be a psychological defence against feeling depressed, rather than a 'brain disorder'. When asked to name words in a test, people who have recovered from manic depression find it harder to say words that are related to depression than ones related to euphoria. Although they claim they are fine, in fact they often seem to be suffering from low-grade depression. Further studies suggest that depressive words are emotionally troubling to them, and they have large fluctuations in their self-esteem. When followed up, it turns out that the greater the number of hidden signs of depression they have when ostensibly well, the greater the risk of the illness recurring. During their manic phase, despite the euphoria, patients are very similar to depressives in their scores on some tests. The frantic activity of mania is a desperate attempt to distract the self away from a depressive core; it can take the form of a frenetic battle to replace low self-esteem with achievement or activity.

Paranoia is a common symptom of schizophrenia, and it seems to be anything but the purely mechanical malfunction that conventional psychiatry deems it. Symptoms appear to have meaning. Paranoiacs the world over are expert at taking credit for positive events but avoiding blame for negative ones. When some were given a computer game to play, the true result of which they had no control over, they claimed all the credit for winning but declared that it was rigged (quite rightly, in fact!) if they lost. Depressed patients, in contrast, took barely more credit for winning than for losing.

Taken overall, from today's scientific perspective, Bowie was absolutely right to suppose himself to be capable of making his distress intelligible and to treat it as something he might be able to manage through his own unusual form of music and performance therapy. The major preoccupation throughout his albums in the early 1970s was madness.

The B side of his 1969 'Space Oddity' – his first Top Ten single – was called 'The Wild Eyed Boy From Freecloud', about a boy imprisoned in a village and awaiting the hangman. The boy is declared mad by the villagers, and he struggles to decide whether it is he or the villagers who are the crazy ones.

The ideas in the song reflect those of the then-popular psychoanalyst Ronald Laing. An avid and scholarly reader throughout his adult life, Bowie was aware of them. Laing had written several books maintaining that families drive children mad but, more than this, that the craziness of much of society is far greater than that of the schizophrenic* (Laing had asked whether the schizophrenic who believes he has a nuclear bomb inside him is crazier than the country that possesses one.)

Along with 'The Wild Eyed Boy', the *Space Oddity* album (first released with the title *David Bowie*, in 1969) included several other songs referring to madness. Bowie said that 'Unwashed And Somewhat Slightly Dazed' was ostensibly about 'a boy whose girlfriend thinks he is socially inferior'. It refers to a period when Bowie was so scruffy that he recalled being given 'funny stares' in the street. He was deeply upset at having been jilted by Hermione Farthingale (described in the third song on the album, 'Letter to Hermione'). He sings of himself as a phallus in pig-tails and as rotting tissue that rats chew. He also warns: 'Look out, I'm raving mad.' In 'Janine', the first song on the second side of the album, Bowie speaks of things inside his head that even he cannot face.

The next album, *The Man Who Sold The World* (produced in the spring and summer of 1970), continues these themes. The instrumental music was composed and recorded first, and the producer, Tony Visconti, became increasingly worried that there were no lyrics. Desperate for them, he issued an ultimatum, demanding they be provided within three days. Bowie had always arrived with the words ready early in the proceedings. This proved to be the first of many albums where he would write the lyrics at the last minute, very rapidly, in a flow of consciousness. They seem to have come straight from his unconscious.

The song after which the album is named begins with a children's nursery rhyme, conjuring up images of a mysterious man. The man comes and goes, representing both death (the grim reaper) and another part of himself, in which he has become a divided personality (Ronald Laing's first book, about schizophrenia, was entitled *The Divided Self* *). Since madness is social death, the two intertwine easily.

In an interview after the song's release, Bowie said:

'The subject-matter was very telling for me – it was all family problems.'

Speaking subsequently about a cover version of the song (oddly enough, by the popular singer Lulu) he commented that he would not wish the song on her because it was about the 'devils and angels' within himself. Interestingly, though, through all the man's travails in 'The Man Who Sold The World', Bowie sings that he never lost control. This prefigured the period to come, between early 1974 and March 1976, when he was taking so much cocaine that he became sporadically delusional and paranoid. Despite this, he never did lose control, either of himself or of his career.

Bowie had already sung, on the *Space Oddity* album ('Cygnet Committee'), of screwing up his half-brother, Terry, or he would get you in the end. Now, in the song 'Black Country Rock', he sang of a nightmare dream in which he might tear his half-brother's flesh. Bowie is making explicit his feeling that his success was at Terry's expense.

The song 'All The Madmen' is specifically devoted to Terry's madness. In 1972, Bowie stated that it 'was written for my brother and it's all about my brother'. In 1967 Terry had hallucinated Jesus Christ; since then he had been living at Cane Hill mental hospital, although he did come to stay with Bowie while Bowie was making the album. One of the people living with Bowie recalled that Bowie '*was* bothered about him', confirmed by his first wife, Angie (Mary Angela Barnett), who also said that when they met, the brothers were still very close, as they had been when Bowie was small. Others living there recalled being careful to avoid making comments that might trigger Bowie's fears about Terry and about his own sanity: jokes about 'loonies' were forbidden.

'All The Madmen' begins by telling how, day after day, they send his friends away, to a cold and grey mansion. This is on a hill high on the edge of the town – as was Cane Hill. Perhaps partly reflecting Laing's idea that the sane are mad and the mad sane, the song maintains that the asylum residents are quite as sane as Bowie. By implication, though, this also means that he is fit for a mental hospital.

The song is a condemnation of incarcerating the mad, reflecting Bowie's view expressed in an interview with *The Times* newspaper the previous year. The song is also about the problem for him of having to put his brother out of his mind, mentally locking him up and throwing away the key. This is, to quite an extent, what he did for several years. Although Terry visited him, he did not visit Terry in hospital.

The feeling that 'it's either him or me' was present in comments he made to his cousin Kristina in New York in 1971. She reported that one of the puzzles for Bowie was 'why he was chosen and Terry was left. He could have been Terry – when you come that close to it.' This issue was explicitly addressed in a song on Bowie's subsequent *Hunky Dory* album, 'The Bewlay Brothers', which, he told Kristina, was about Terry. It speaks of a brother lying on some rocks, possibly dead, how he might be 'you'.

Bowie was working incredibly hard during the 1970s, distorted by cocaine from early 1974 to March 1976, and between 1972 and 1982 he made virtually no attempts to contact his ailing half-brother or to give him any help. In marked contrast, he was extremely caring and solicitous to Iggy Pop, whom he saw in some respects as an older brother, one of the very few people to whom he remained close for a long period (until his forties, his intimate professional or personal relationships were nearly all short-lived). As well as nursing Iggy out of addictions that had taken him close to psychosis, a few years later Bowie resurrected Iggy's career by being the producer of his best-selling album. For a subsequent Iggy album Bowie chose a cover picture that had connotations of Terry*.

Although too much can be made of Bowie's guilt about his half-brother, in 1982 Bowie recognised its extent. The character Celliers, whom he played in the film *Merry Christmas, Mr Lawrence*, had a brother whom Celliers does not save from a cruel initiation ceremony at school. Bowie said of the role that:

> 'I found in Celliers all too many areas of guilt and shortcomings that are part of me. I feel tremendous guilt because I grew so apart from my family. I hardly ever see my mother and I have a half-brother I don't see any more. It was my fault we grew apart and it is painful – but somehow there is no going back.'

By this time, Bowie had returned to recreational drug use rather than its abuse, and he could see his situation more clearly. But he knew well that, back in 1976, when he had nearly slipped into madness, he had been all too similar to Terry: personally unkempt, believing he was being visited by nonexistent entities, paranoid, and at times seeing himself as a Messiah, with a god-given role.

Bowie described *Hunky Dory*, his next album, as a 'very worried' one. It was created during the first half of 1971. While many listeners hummed along to its frequently upbeat, sunny sound, it contained several discussions of his fear of madness. As so often in his lyrics, he rarely chose the obvious rhymes or followed where the narrative seemed to be leading.

The song 'Changes' explains how 'time may change me' – but, instead of continuing that he cannot change time, he says he cannot *trace* it, a less obvious idea. He struggles in the song to define himself, so that he turns himself to face himself and fails to find him. As in 'The Man Who Sold The World', where he passes a stranger on some stairs who could be death or madness, he exhorts us to turn and face the stranger (a pun – the stranger that you may be to yourself, as well as the stranger experiences entailed in changing).

Strangers appeared again in 'Oh! You Pretty Things', another song whose cheery, carefree tone and some of whose lyrics could have the unsuspecting teenage audience feeling liberated from parents (whom, they are told, they are driving insane). In fact, not only are the strangers present, there is a specific reference that resonates with his half-brother's schizophrenic episode and his own fears of a similar fate. Terry had looked up and seen Jesus Christ in a blaze of light, telling him he was chosen. Now Bowie saw a crack in the sky and a hand reaching down to him.

In 1976, Bowie said of the song:

'The crack in the sky, the hand coming through the crack in the sky . . . a lot of the songs in fact do deal with some kind of schizophrenia . . . and 'Oh! You Pretty Things' was one of them.'

Next comes 'Life On Mars?', which starts off with a plangent melody and some lines that refer to the only woman Bowie had fallen in love with: Hermione Farthingale, including her mousy hair and the God-awfulness of the shortness of their affair. The chorus ends by asking whether there is life on Mars. In his 1970s work, Bowie repeatedly refers to space and aliens, outer space often used to refer to inner space, our mind. The song 'Space Oddity' was taken by many to be 'about' the experience of losing your self, and of being unable to return to a safe emotional base; some also read it as an account of drug-taking, particularly heroin, a drug that Bowie had dabbled in. Many of Bowie's lyrics are, of course, deliberately intended to be 'about' more than one thing at a time: his work is littered with puns.

A major worry in *Hunky Dory* is that his creativity is finite and could disappear at any moment, for his lyrics seemed to be coming from nowhere. In the case of 'Oh! You Pretty Things', for example, he recalled that he had woken up at 4 am, and 'I had to get out of bed and just play it to get it out of me so that I could get back to sleep again'. That his magic could suddenly leave him is discussed in various ways in subsequent songs on the album, especially 'Quicksand', where the actually ultra-creative singer laments the fact that he lacks the power, sinking in the quicksand of his thought.

An eager devotee of the work of the stream-of-consciousness writer William Burroughs, Bowie was deliberate in creating non-sequitur lyrics. Much later in life, he explained that he liked to 'purposely fracture everything' and that if they made 'too much sense', he would 'fracture' further. In the BBC documentary *Cracked Actor*, filmed in 1974 and screened in 1975, he demonstrated how he would write sentences on a piece of foolscap, cut up the individuals words or phrases and randomly shuffle them. Perhaps this fracturing was partly to tantalise his listeners and part of his skill as a creative impresario, as well as an artist. But there is another intriguing component to the incoherence.

As Bowie must have known from talking with Terry after his breakdown and from witnessing, while still a small boy, the madness of his Aunt Una, when people become psychotic, they can be incomprehensible, speaking in what is called schizophrenese. This entails chains of apparently unconnected words, puns, extreme language with extravagant adjectives, and alarming images of disturbing subjects like sex and violence. Conventional psychiatry dismisses such diction as the meaningless nonsense of a disordered brain, caused by damage to neural networks or key brain mechanisms. But there is no reliable evidence of a diseased brain. If a thousand or ten thousand brains are randomly chosen and scanned, it is currently impossible to use the results to predict which belong to the schizophrenics. In fact, given that we now know that most schizophrenia is caused by severe maltreatment, it is safe to assume that their words are highly meaningful attempts to give voice to trauma.

Much of Bowie's work during the 1970s can be viewed through that prism. The paranoid delusions, grandiose fantasies and hallucinations of the mad litter his thinking as he hops from one more or less crazy idea to the next. His sexual imagery is very rarely tender; it is nearly always greedy, desperate, angry. He frequently describes severe violence, images of children smashed on the ground, of blood and gore. It is as if he is evoking schizophrenic experiences through the disconnection of his lyrics, perhaps enabling him to remain just on the right side of sanity when not singing or creating them. By giving vent to his crazy ideas in crazy words, the creation and performance of the lyrics protect him from being crazy.

Certainly, he believed himself to be close to that state during the period when *Cracked Actor* was filmed. Watching the documentary again in 1987, he said of his former self that:

> 'I was so blocked . . . so stoned . . . I'm amazed I came out of that period, honest. When I see that now I cannot believe I survived it. I was so close to really throwing myself away physically, completely.'

He may have perceived himself as simply creating art at the time, but it is also possible that the subtle manner in which he concealed his meanings from his listeners was also an attempt to protect himself from too clear a picture. He wanted to know – and then again, perhaps he did not. The ambiguity may have felt safer.

At another level, too, he was surely seeking – as most artists do – to draw his listeners in and force them to make an effort to understand him. He is always at great pains to give us just enough of a sense of a narrative to keep us listening. He uses the lure of the melodies, the power of the instrumental arrangements and the clever production to do so. He put enormous effort into being physically appealing, attracting and intriguing us. He may not have felt either loved or understood by his parents, especially by his mother – but he wanted a relationship with his fans in which, having been seduced, they sensed his desperation and his chaotic inner world. He wanted to feel understood as well as loved.

His lyrics may have been an inspired way to cope with the possibility of his becoming speech-disordered. Studies show clearly that speech disorder in schizophrenics is more likely if the subject of conversation is emotionally charged*. When asked to talk about sad rather than happy memories, the speech becomes measurably more disordered; the more personal the subject-matter, the more so. By coping with his distress through his poetic lyrics, it is very possible Bowie may well have been able to remain relatively coherent when not singing them. When spoken in everyday life, the words of some poems would seem like speech disorder. Some poetry can be regarded as an author's speech disorder by other means.

In the three albums produced between 1969 and 1971 (*Space Oddity*, *The Man Who Sold The World* and *Hunky Dory*), Bowie was in the grip of a fear that the madness of his aunts and half-brother was caused by a genetic defect that would afflict him. The music also expressed his truly splintered, fractured inner life. This work of self-expression helped him to stay in one piece. But the albums did not produce the fame he sought, nor did they release him from his terrors, although they were eventually to become regarded by many as fine works of art (particularly *Hunky Dory*). What was needed was something else, if he was to fulfil his aspiration to be a world-famous rock star and if he was to be able to transcend the legacy of his family politics. It took *The Rise And Fall Of Ziggy Stardust And The Spiders From Mars* to achieve those breakthroughs.

TWO

'Bad seed'

In 1976, David Bowie (born David Jones) described his family: 'Most of them are nutty – in, just out of, or going into an institution. Or dead.'

Bowie's comments to journalists have to be treated with considerable caution. He was often playful and mischievous, sometimes sarcastic or ironic, and occasionally fantastical. However, there is good reason to suppose that, while there was a measure of hyperbole, he was accurate in saying this of his family. Three of his maternal aunts spent time in mental hospitals, two of them diagnosed as schizophrenic, the third as manic-depressive, and Terry, his half-brother, spent many years in a mental hospital, also with a diagnosis of schizophrenia. The mental illness of his aunts and half-brother was to play an important role in the drama of David Bowie's life.

His mother's name was Peggy, and the madness ran on her side of the family. Born in 1913, she was the oldest of six siblings, five of them girls. In order to understand David Bowie's concern with madness, you need a brief sketch of her parents (his maternal grandparents) and his aunts.

THE BURNS FAMILY

Margaret and Jimmy Burns

Jimmy Burns, Bowie's maternal grandfather, was a man of proud and upright bearing, with jet-black hair and a magnificent waxed moustache. During the First World War he survived four years at the front, and the tales of his heroism were retold to Bowie in his childhood, becoming the inspiration for several of his early songs (most notably, 'Little Bombardier'). By the end of the war, Burns was one of only three dozen men from his regiment who had survived the whole war from the start. He was also that rare thing, a working-class foot soldier who was promoted to the rank of officer, although the war ended before he was able to serve as one.

In 1912 he had married Margaret, the daughter of a professional soldier, and they set up house in Southborough, Kent. They had six children, five of them daughters. The marriage was not a happy one. He was an extrovert, fun-loving Catholic, she was a relatively austere Anglican who did not enjoy displays of overt affection. Fond of demonstrating his physical prowess, he liked to pick Margaret up by the waist. Embarrassed by such public intimacy, she would demand to be put down. One of her daughters, Pat, later reported that the only way she could get Margaret to embrace her was to put her arms around her mother, take her arms and pull them round. When Pat would sit on her father's lap listening to his stories, Margaret would object that she was 'too old for that sort of thing'.

Neighbours of the Burns recalled Margaret as aloof and incommunicative. She was socially ambitious, and when her husband returned from the war and was unable to find employment, she felt resentful that her station in life was relatively low. For three years, Jimmy was reduced to busking with a clarinet for money – he was a keen musician, teaching most of his children to play a variety of instruments. She gradually withdrew into herself, spending much of her time reading Shakespeare and Jane Austen. She also took up poetry, carrying a small notebook in which she inscribed ideas. Her poems have a startling similarity to the themes of some of Bowie's early lyrics. Tales of love and regret, parting and nostalgia, they reveal her loneliness and belief in the therapeutic power of fantasy. Like Bowie's early work, they dwelt on the land of make-believe and the play through which children express themselves.

Peggy, Bowie's mother

While Mrs Burns explored the world of literature, her daughters, as they grew up, sought more earthly pursuits, starting with the oldest, Peggy. Aged 22 in 1935, she was strikingly good-looking. She took a post as a nanny to the owners of a hotel in Tunbridge Wells and in her spare time modelled corsets and lingerie at a dress shop.

Among the staff at the hotel where she nannied was Jack Rosemberg, a barman. He was the son of a prosperous Parisian fur dealer, and his Latin good looks and debonair manner bewitched Peggy. Ignorance of contraception was common at that time, and having fallen in love with Jack, she fell pregnant. After the initial rage of Peggy's father and her mother's tears, Rosemberg was introduced to them and, under considerable pressure, agreed to marriage. Shortly afterwards, he disappeared.

Peggy bore a son, Terry, but returned to work six months later, leaving Terry to be cared for by Margaret. While Jimmy dandled him on his knee and some of Peggy's sisters pitched in, it seems unlikely that Margaret would have felt huge enthusiasm for her illegitimate grandson. Her airs and graces, her desire for social superiority, took a knock in an era when single mothers were not socially acceptable. But the stigma of Peggy's illegitimate child was only the beginning.

Two years after the arrival of Terry, the Second World War broke out, and misfortune followed misfortune for the Burns family: three of the daughters went mad.

Una

The first to go mad was Una, their fourth daughter, with long golden hair and a snub nose, aged 19 when the war began. She was posted to Aldershot to work for the NAAFI, the military supply organisation. In 1941 she fell in love with Kurt Paulsen, a handsome Canadian soldier. She became pregnant, bearing a daughter, Kristina. She lied to her parents that they had married, so the Burns' were at first content, and Una lived with Paulsen in Guilford. But Margaret became suspicious, and it emerged that Paulsen had a wife and family in Canada. For a time, Margaret assumed that he was a bigamist, because Una continued to maintain that they were married.

After Paulsen left to take part in the 1944 Normandy landings, the strain on Una of maintaining the fiction was too much, and she broke down, spending several months in a mental hospital, diagnosed as schizophrenic. When she returned home, her family were shocked at how dishevelled and unkempt she had become. Her moods were febrile, sometimes hostile and aggressive, at others depressed and introverted. She heard voices and would sometimes speak in a truncated, confusing fashion.

Margaret was mystified by Una's condition. She had not been informed that Una was suffering paranoid ideas of being persecuted and having visions of heaven and hell. Finding no solace at home, Una returned to Guilford with her daughter. She stayed in lodging houses, finding occasional jobs, always hoping that Paulsen would return. She never saw him again and was in and out of mental hospitals for the rest of her life.

Nora

The war proved equally cataclysmic for Nora, the second-born in the family. Aged 24 when it began, she became engaged to a Welsh soldier who was subsequently captured and became a prisoner of war. She vowed to wait for his return, but when he did so, he broke off their engagement, and Nora was crushed. She sat around at home chain-smoking and having tantrums. Margaret explained her misery as a case of 'bad nerves'.

Nora then had a love affair with a Polish refugee, emaciated by malnutrition and startlingly unstable, called Jan. Nora lived with him for a time in London, and then, at the end of the war, she returned with him to Poland, a nation that had been devastated and was now part of the Soviet Union. The bitter cold and desperate shortage of food soon led to Nora heading home.

On her return, she had severely deteriorated: screaming, breaking windows and having terrible rages. She was admitted to a mental hospital and was diagnosed as suffering from manic depression. Margaret signed a consent form for a lobotomy to be performed, an operation that cut the linkages between the frontal lobes and the rest of the brain. While Nora's irascibility did seem to be doused by the operation, she remained severely depressed and was moved to a mental hospital.

Vivienne

Margaret Burns must have been deeply humiliated by these events. Two of her daughters had had illegitimate children, both were hospitalised with mental illnesses. But if that were not enough, her fifth daughter, Vivienne, was also to be claimed by what seemed to Margaret like a curse. The only daughter to have inherited her father's jet-black hair, Vivienne was small, witty and vivacious. Aged 17 at the start of the war, in 1944 she became a GI bride and emigrated with her husband to his home, near Washington, DC. However, in 1957 she also suffered a schizophrenic breakdown. Years later, pondering the misfortunes of her family, she still spoke in the fractured, disjointed speech pattern of someone with schizophrenia.

A whole family cursed

By the end of the war, Margaret Burns herself showed many signs of being highly disturbed. She found it hard to express emotion or affection, disliked physical contact with others, had profound status envy, was isolated and remote, and showed increasing hostility and violence towards others. Nowadays, she would probably be diagnosed as having a borderline personality disorder, only one point away from madness on the spectrum of sanity.

That she should have been so distressed was partly an understandable reaction to these terrible misfortunes and to the fact that in 1946 her husband developed leukaemia and died. But many of her distressed traits long predated the calamities. There were those in the family who felt that the way she had cared for her children was the reason half of them had developed major mental illnesses.

After the war, Peggy – who married in 1946 and gave birth to Bowie – had a furious row with Margaret, blaming all the family's misfortunes on her. Her mother reacted by claiming that Peggy had been a 'bad seed' from the outset – that she had had defective genes. Margaret expanded that explanation further when she declared that the whole family was cursed. She decreed that the curse would only end when all members of the family were dead.

Forty years later, her family members still recalled Margaret's curse. Bowie was aware of this and, as a child and young adult, was confronted by the madness of Terry and of Una. On many occasions he publicly stated that he feared madness as a fate, and, indeed, during his cocaine period, he did cross the line into delusion and sporadically psychotic functioning.

THE CAUSES OF PSYCHOSIS (SCHIZOPHRENIA AND BIPOLAR DISORDER)

It is a fact that blood relatives of schizophrenics are at greater risk of suffering themselves[*]. Having a schizophrenic parent – especially the mother – represents the greatest risk, but schizophrenia in siblings and other close relatives is also of relevance, though to decreasing degrees. The overall effect, however, is cumulative. So in Bowie's case, with three aunts and a half-brother who were schizophrenic, he was considerably more at risk than someone with no schizophrenic relatives.

The psychiatric establishment frequently offers the fact that schizophrenia runs in families as evidence that the problems are caused by genes. They ignore – or have never considered – the fact that it could just as much be proof of the role of nurture as of nature. Patterns of parenting could be causing the problem – patterns that may have nothing to do with genes.

There is strong evidence that doctors are brainwashed into the biogenetic explanation of mental illness and that this has negative consequences*. If relatives, professionals or people with psychoses believe that explanation, then the prognosis for the psychotic is worse. So the row between Peggy and Margaret about why so many of the family had become psychotic was of more than academic interest; in themselves, the beliefs Margaret held were toxic. Bowie was to wrestle with this issue for many years: Was he condemned by genes to madness? Why had three of his aunts and his half-brother suffered it?

Research in the last twenty-five years supports the idea that the transmission is through nurture, not nature*. It is a fact that no differences in specific bits of genetic material (DNA) have been demonstrated to play a significant role* ('significant' meaning around 20% or more of the reason one person is schizophrenic and another is not). That no such significant role for genes has been shown to exist for any psychological traits, including intelligence and depression as well as schizophrenia, is not disputed by geneticists. It is a fact dubbed 'missing heritability' and is baldly admitted in the most recent reviews of the evidence, even by researchers who say they believe that genes still will be found*. It is true that some differences in DNA have been correlated with schizophrenia. However, when all these are added together, they can explain only 1–5% of the risk* – so negligible as to be of no importance.

Further evidence against a genetic basis for schizophrenia comes from studies involving identical twins. These have shown that, on average, of 100 schizophrenics with an identical twin, 51 of the identikits will not have the illness*. All the twin pairs have identical genes, so in the 51 pairs where one is schizophrenic and the other is not, genes cannot possibly be the cause of the illness – both would have it if genes were critical.

Everything said here about schizophrenia goes for bipolar disorder*: the same lack of any evidence that specific differences in genes play a significant role in causing it.

It really does seem as if genes may play little or no part in explaining why three of Margaret's daughters developed psychoses and her other three offspring did not. In which case, what did explain it?

A definitive analysis of the 41 best studies of the impact of childhood adversity on the risk of psychosis (meaning mostly schizophrenia and bipolar disorder) was published in 2012*. The kinds of adversities tested were childhood sexual and physical abuse; emotional abuse (such as over-control, stigmatisation, favouritism); physical and emotional neglect; bullying; and parental death. Regardless of the methods of study used, the analysis showed that childhood adversity increased threefold the risk of psychosis. Similar results were found by another recent analysis of 25 studies specifically devoted to the relationship of childhood adversity to schizophrenia*: three times greater risk where there had been childhood adversity.

As the number of adversities rises, so does the risk*. At the extreme, one study reported that if you had been subjected to five kinds of maltreatment, you were 193 times more likely to be psychotic than if you had suffered none*. The relative contribution of each kind of maltreatment has also been analysed* and, perhaps surprisingly, emotional abuse – not sexual abuse – turns out to be the most psychosis-inducing, increasing the risk twelvefold*. This is significant because, as we shall see, there is considerable evidence that Margaret was emotionally abusive and that Bowie's mother, Peggy, was too. In terms of expression of love, the temperature of the home she provided for him was said to have been 'subzero'.

There are likely to be other subtle forms of maltreatment involved, which have not been properly measured. For example, Ronald Laing, whose family case histories of maltreatment were widely read in the 1960s*, suggested that parents can 'double-bind' their children, so that whatever the child does is wrong. For example, a mother comes to visit her son at a mental hospital. He approaches her to give her a kiss, but then her body freezes and she backs off. As he moves back, she asks, 'Darling, aren't you going to give your mother a kiss?' Whatever the son does, kiss or not kiss, he is in the wrong – it's enough to drive you crazy.

There is evidence indicating early origins of the vulnerability to psychosis. Many theorists have proposed that a lack of responsiveness and love, and erratic or intrusive care create a weak sense of self in infants and toddlers*. In accord with this, there is convincing evidence that dissociation – a detachment from yourself, especially your feelings, that is a key symptom of psychosis – is much more likely in early adulthood if care before age 2 has been poor*. There are direct links between early insecurity as a toddler, resulting from inadequate care, and later schizophrenia*. It seems very likely that if a large enough sample of people are followed from before birth (the foetal period has also been implicated in psychosis*) into adulthood, it will emerge that early experience is a crucial factor in creating vulnerability to psychosis.

Perhaps the strongest single clue to this is the simple fact that schizophrenic mothers are twice as likely as schizophrenic fathers to have a schizophrenic offspring*. This fact has been completely ignored by nearly all scientists, yet it is highly significant. The unfortunate and pejorative term 'refrigerator mothers' was coined in the 1960s to refer to mothers of schizophrenics. Genetically minded observers have referred to this label repeatedly in attempts to blacken research proving that maternal care can, indeed, be a major cause of the problem. But in saying that Margaret may have been the main cause of the schizophrenia of her offspring, blame is not the issue: what is relevant is an understanding of her and the likelihood that she too will have been subjected to maltreatment.

Of course, it could be argued that children of schizophrenic mothers, rather than of fathers, are twice as likely to have the illness, because genes are passed down the maternal line. But the Human Genome Project findings make this improbable*. Mothers do most of the early care of infants and toddlers. A mother who is schizophrenic is much less likely to be able to provide the responsiveness, love and security that under-3s need*. This is not to say that fathers play no part, especially as they are much more often the sexual abusers, where this has taken place. But it seems that emotional abuse creates the greatest risk, and this is more likely to be from the mother – if nothing else, because mothers spend more time with small children than do fathers.

There is growing evidence that in terms of symptoms, specific maltreatments have specific outcomes*. In many respects, schizophrenics resemble people with post-traumatic stress disorder (PTSD). Soldiers who have been through horrific experiences in war zones or ordinary people who endure gruesome accidents often find themselves re-experiencing the horrors in ways that seem as real as the original trauma, just as dreams seem real to us. They sometimes hallucinate; they believe themselves to be in places or times that are not the ones they are 'really' in, and they become very fearful, to the point of paranoia. It is much the same for survivors of childhood adversity.

The clinical psychologist John Read points out that there is growing evidence that the way in which childhood adversity causes psychosis is by forcing the child to develop patterns of coping that, in later life, emerge as psychotic symptoms. Any of the adversities are liable to make children insecure – not sure of whether they can trust people to love them. Frequently they have to suppress their emotions to avoid falling apart – if you have been repeatedly beaten at home, for example, then, when you get to school, you cannot simply sob all day. Instead, you may develop a hard shell or become aggressive. Of the defences, dissociation seems to be the most important. When being sexually abused, for example, children often report that they have had the sensation that they were not there, up to and including imaging themselves to be on the ceiling watching what is being done to their body. Such experiences can lead to a tendency to put oneself in dangerous situations and relationships*.

In a recent review of the evidence*, Read offers what is now a widely accepted model of the way childhood adversity affects brain development to create a heightened sensitivity to stresses in adult life, making psychosis more likely. Stresses trigger psychosis, which changes the brain and the patterns of brainwaves*. Adults who have had relatively benign childhoods can withstand such stresses.

There is a long list of alterations in the chemistry of the brains of children who have been subjected to adversity. Very much the same chemical deficits are found in schizophrenic adults. Read points out that it is a mistake to characterise schizophrenia as a brain disorder. Rather, schizophrenics were maltreated children whose bodies became used to stress, showing up in physical measures thereof. For example, the chemical system that is developed to deal with threat by fight or flight is more sensitive in schizophrenics. That is hardly surprising if, as children, they were threatened repeatedly with physical or sexual assaults, or with emotionally abusive hostility or intrusiveness. When you add in that maltreated children become teens and adults who are more likely to get into risky situations or lifestyles, it increases the likelihood that they will be hypersensitive to threat. The same goes for the reward systems in the body, such as the hormone dopamine*.

Read points out that the crucial factor in causing psychosis that runs in families is childhood adversity, not genes. While there is some evidence that such adversity switches certain genes on or off, this is still largely limited to studies of animals. Even if that theory proves to be correct, it will only add to the evidence that early care directly impacts on the body, that the maltreatment is the cause, and that bodily changes (including whether genes are turned on or not) are an effect of this. Whether maltreatment is passed down the generations by the way it impacts on genes remains to be seen. What now seems very likely is that it is inherited through the way parents care for children, and how those children subsequently care for their own offspring.

In the light of all this evidence, it seems highly probable that the reason that three of Margaret's children became psychotic is that they suffered some of the adversities described above, whereas the other three did not. This is not as odd as it may sound. Children in a family are treated remarkably differently by their parents, and the amount of adversity experienced, where this is present, will vary. Hence, studies of identical twins, where one was maltreated and not the other, do indeed show a greater likelihood of schizophrenia* in the maltreated twin. (The same has been shown for attention deficit hyperactivity disorder*.)

We do not know in what ways Una, Nora and Vivienne were cared for differently compared with their three siblings who did not develop psychoses. In the case of Una, it could be supposed that having an illegitimate child at a time when that was stigmatised was a trigger. But Peggy also had not one, but two illegitimate children without becoming psychotic. Una was clearly more vulnerable. The evidence above offers a menu of childhood adversities that could have caused this. That one of these daughters was diagnosed as bipolar does not mean that childhood maltreatment was not the primary cause – numerous studies also show a relationship between that specific form of psychosis and childhood maltreatment*.

In what we do know about Margaret, the fact that she was a detached woman, perhaps dissociated, stands out. She was socially and emotionally insecure, highly averse to physical contact. Children, particularly young children, need to be hugged and cuddled. It is possible that Margaret was less able to tune in to her second, fourth and fifth children (Nora, Una and Vivienne) when they were small than to the others. It is also possible that other people in the household gave the non-psychotic offspring the attention and love that provided them with resilience against the distress resulting from having a cold mother.

Another possibility has to be considered: that the three daughters who became psychotic had been sexually abused by someone, possibly within the family (and nearly all sexual abuse is carried out by men).

Above all else, though, it is what happened to Peggy's illegitimate son, Terry, that makes it probable that it was Margaret who was the key cause of the psychoses in her offspring. From the age of 6 months, Terry was cared for by Margaret – and this may be a highly significant indication of Margaret's mothering: Terry went on to join his aunts in becoming psychotic.

THREE

The unfavoured brother

If the madness of Bowie's aunts persuaded him that he was at high risk himself, that of Terry, his half-brother, also profoundly influenced his life and music. Bowie's own statements, and the lyrics of some of his songs, show that he felt guilt at being favoured over Terry during their childhood and, subsequently, guilt at not being more supportive as his brother slipped into madness. Crucially, Terry's madness – more than that of his aunts – convinced Bowie that Margaret's curse had substance.

The cause of Terry's disturbance can be traced to three main experiences. The first was the poor quality of care provided by his grandmother Margaret, his main carer when he was small. The second was the peripatetic nature of that care, as he bounced between the homes of his mother, his grandmother and, in later years, his Aunt Pat (the youngest of Margaret's children). The third was the strong antipathy shown by his step-father, John – Bowie's biological father.

Terry's biological father, Jack Rosemberg, the man Peggy later called 'the love of my life', had departed soon after he heard of the pregnancy. However, soon after his birth in 1937, Peggy had sent a picture of Terry to Rosemberg's parents in Paris, and they offered to take him off her hands. Peggy refused.

When Terry was still small, during the war, Rosemberg suddenly reappeared, now a member of the Free French Forces. Peggy was not at home, and Margaret invited him in. He pulled out a wad of cash and offered to take Terry away, right there and then. Although Rosemberg almost begged, Margaret refused to agree without Peggy's permission (though she did take the cash). Rosemberg left, never to be seen again, but his existence not only endured for Peggy (she never felt the same passion for Bowie's father), it did so, too, for Terry: as a teenager and adult, he carried a battered picture of Rosemberg – whom he had only met on this one occasion in his early childhood – in his wallet. Had Rosemberg taken him, he would, at least, have been wanted and might well never have become psychotic. For although Peggy refused to let Terry go, she showed little inclination to mother him herself.

Speaking of Peggy's relationship with Terry, his Aunt Pat later said, 'I never saw her kiss him or put her arms round his shoulders, or touch him, nothing.' After the first six months, Margaret was literally left holding the baby. But she did not want him either. The additional burden of a grandson cannot have been welcome, given that she had had six children of her own (the youngest of whom, Pat, was then 9). Her humiliation, given her social pretensions and the strong stigma associated with illegitimacy, must also have played a major role. Rejection was something he was subsequently to be exposed to from his mother and his step-father.

Being unwanted is a predictor of maltreatment for children, in general, and doubles the risk of schizophrenia, in particular. In one study, 220 Czechoslovakian children were identified whose mothers had twice asked for abortions but been refused. The mothers were less likely to breastfeed them than wanted children. At age 9, the children were doing worse at school, were less diligent and were prone to explosive irritability and defensiveness*. The problems were still present at age 15, with the children reporting a lack of positive interest in them from their mothers.

Babies whose mothers had negative feelings about them at the age of 1 month are 18 times more likely to be emotionally insecure aged 30–40*, and there is evidence of a greater risk of schizophrenia in later life. Two studies have measured the attitudes of pregnant mothers to having a child, including whether it was unwanted or a mistake. Although these are not as strong an indication of unwantedness as actively seeking an abortion – and doubtless many of the mothers changed their feelings on seeing their newborn – there was double the risk of schizophrenia for the child when it grew up*. There have been similar findings in connection with adults who are semi-schizophrenic – having been unwanted makes this much more likely*.

Perhaps most critically, Margaret was very far from being a warm mother. Kristina (Una's illegitimate daughter) was also cared for by Margaret at various times in childhood. She described Margaret as 'a very cruel woman who took her anger out on everyone around her'. Once, when Terry was rebuked by Margaret for some misdemeanour, he smirked out of nervousness. Kristina recalled that 'Nanny [Margaret] said "go on, laugh again", and he nervously did so. She smacked him across the ear and said, "that'll teach you to laugh at me".' On another occasion, when he was still small, Terry accidentally smeared some faeces on the lavatory seat, which was too high up for him to reach easily. Kristina recalled that 'Nanny took him out and rubbed his nose in it. He was very upset by that and cried a lot.' Perhaps as a result of repeatedly being subjected to this kind of emotional abuse, Kristina recalls him as having been 'very quiet and sensitive, he didn't laugh a lot'. As a first-hand account of how Margaret could mother, it gives some clues as to what may have induced psychosis in her three natural daughters, since, as discussed above, emotional abuse is the maltreatment that most strongly correlates with schizophrenia.

His aunts remember Terry more as exceptionally good-looking, with blue eyes and an angelic face. Pat remembers that his grandfather did lavish attention on him, as did she. She taught him to read, taking him on her lap, using a comic album.

His mother Peggy, by contrast, was an unreliable presence. Her main contribution was to buy him expensive clothes, like Fair Isle sweaters, tweed trousers and the best leather shoes. She contributed no money to the more mundane matters of his bed and board. Peggy would turn up during the rest of the war on the arms of a succession of soldiers, who were introduced as his 'uncle'. This may well have led to him being confused as to who was his primary carer. Where did he belong, in the menagerie of this large household?

In 1943, one of Peggy's boyfriends (in this case, a married man) got her pregnant, and she had a second illegitimate child, a daughter. Margaret was incensed and this time refused to have anything to do with the baby. After three months, Peggy gave the infant away to be adopted.

In 1945, with Peggy now aged 32 and working as a wait-ress, John Jones, who was to be Bowie's father, appeared on the scene. After a short courtship, she married him, and they eventually moved together into a house in Brixton. Terry, now aged 10 and still living with Margaret, would occasion-ally visit, and Peggy was eager for him to join them. An exceptional pupil, Terry had passed the entrance exam into a good school in Tonbridge (interestingly, there is a higher incidence of schizophrenia and of suicide in high academic achievers*, which may be the result of having to people-please parents*). Perhaps as Margaret was increasingly unstable following the death of her husband, Peggy may have felt this was a good reason to move her son to live with her. That she did not automatically insist on her son doing so at the outset suggests how weak was her bond with him or her sense of obligation. However, she did manage to gain Terry a place at a nearby grammar school in Clapham, and he moved in with his mother and step-father. Alas, his experience of being unwanted, explicitly by Margaret and implicitly by his mother's neglect up to that point, was only heightened by this move.

The greatest problem was that John was aware that Terry's father, Jack Rosemberg, had been the love of Peggy's life. John was a relatively low-key, unglamorous man beside this exotic rival, and deep down he knew that Peggy did not love him to anything like the same degree. Nor did he like being reminded that Peggy had a not inconsiderable 'past'. Unfortunately for Terry, he looked strikingly like the dashing Rosemberg, with his blue eyes, dark hair and broad, confident face. Only when Peggy absolutely insisted did John agree to let Terry move in with them and, subsequently, to having Terry's surname changed by deed poll.

For all of his childhood, John made it clear that he did not want or like his stepson. Terry was a physically clumsy boy, and John mocked him for his lack of athleticism, sneering when he tried to learn to ride a bicycle.

Also living with them for some of the time was Annette, John's daughter from an earlier relationship. She recalled that 'Terry was always in trouble with my father for nothing.' Bowie, by contrast, was 'the be-all and end-all – he was the god of the house'. On getting home from work, John would take Bowie into the sitting room, ask about his day, and tell him about his. Peggy would be in the kitchen, and Terry would disappear off to his room, lonely and disconsolate. Annette said Terry 'could never speak to anyone, he couldn't speak to Daddy, and I don't think he felt free to speak to his mother because of Daddy and David'.

Terry's one confidante was Pat, who, although she was his aunt, was only nine years older. She was a regular visitor and described him as 'a beautiful child, so intelligent and bright'. However, she recalled that following the move to Brixton, 'his spirit was broken in about a year. He would put his arms around my neck when I went to see him there and he had great big blue eyes and he used to whisper to me "I hate him, I hate him, I hate John Jones".'

At least one in ten children report that one of their parents 'really seemed to dislike me or have it in for me'*. There is good evidence that step-parents are more prone to such hostility towards their step-children*. Most telling of all, though, is that there is also evidence that people diagnosed as schizophrenic are more liable to have been victimised, whether at school or at home*.

The only person in Brixton who showed Terry consistent affection was Bowie, who was born in 1947, when Terry was 10. They shared a room, and Bowie would snuggle in his bed on cold mornings. According to Pat, they idolised each other.

Given this unpropitious home life in Brixton, Terry's early academic promise went unfulfilled. His teachers wrote of his intelligence and his expert chess-playing. He was a boxer and in the school cricket team. But none of this was recognised by his discouraging parents. Peggy was never satisfied. Pat recalled that 'she was always criticising, criticising, criticising'. By the age of 14, he was not doing well at school, and he had fainting fits, which meant he had to be brought home. Eventually, John declared that he would not support Terry beyond the age of 15. He left school several months before his 15th birthday, with no qualifications, taking a job as a costings clerk in a publishing company.

In 1953 – Bowie now 7, Terry 17 – Peggy and John bought a house in Bromley. Terry assumed he would move with them, but Peggy found him lodgings in Brixton instead, on the grounds that it would be more convenient for his work. He was a lean, good-looking young man with clean-cut features, who took considerable care over his appearance. Within a short time of being in his new lodgings, Terry punched his homosexual landlord in the face when fighting off sexual advances. Peggy had to allow him to come home to Bromley. But once he was there, his step-father's jealousy and hostility continued, and Terry's isolation was actually amplified.

His main pleasure in Bromley was in playing games with Bowie and Kristina (Una's daughter, who stayed with them off and on throughout her childhood as her mother went in and out of mental hospital). He especially enjoyed playing Monopoly with them and regaling them with stories of their grandfather's war exploits.

Another temporary resident in the household was John's daughter Annette, now aged 16 and training as a nurse. She recalled, about Terry, that 'I don't think that was a very happy time for him, he didn't fit in.' She noticed that if Terry ventured an opinion with John present, he was immediately contradicted. Annette said of Terry's place in the family, 'sometimes with people you feel that if you say something's right, they'll say it's wrong. It was that sort of atmosphere – no actual shouting rows, just edginess.' This account was borne out by Kristina. John actively discouraged signs of affection towards Terry by both Bowie and her, 'even though we both adored him'. The emotional abuse he had suffered at the hands of his grandmother, Margaret, was continuing.

His Aunt Pat noticed how Terry's moods had become volatile. At times he was cheerful and lively, at others deeply pessimistic and dark. He was furious towards his step-father and told her, 'When I grow up, I'm going to kill John.'

As his 18th birthday approached, Terry welcomed the chance presented by National Service to escape. He could have enlisted for only two years but, instead, chose to do three, so keen was he to get away. He told Pat he was 'utterly fed up' and wanted to put as much distance as possible between himself and his family.

Meanwhile, back home, his parents knocked down the wall between the small room Terry had occupied and that of Bowie, to give their favoured son more space. On Terry's return after serving his time in the army, this proved to be a potent symbol of the position he occupied in the family: there was no physical, or emotional, place for him. Arriving home in 1957, he still had his kitbag on his shoulder when Peggy coldly told him that 'you can't stay here'. She did brew him a cup of tea before explaining that there was nowhere for him, that his room was now part of Bowie's. She went on to add, 'Anyway, John doesn't want you here.'

These repeated experiences of rejection are all risk factors for schizophrenia*, starting with Margaret caring for him rather than Peggy, Margaret's cruel emotional and physical abuse (such as the smack for smirking), then John's reluctance to have him in the house and his marginal status in the household. Children who have several different parents or are taken into local authority care are at much greater risk of schizophrenia. But, equally, children who are passed between different carers, with no one really wanting them, are also put at two to three times greater risk*. If parents die, this doubles the risk – but it goes up fivefold if the family is disrupted, such as never having had the biological father live with them, as was the case with Terry*.

Terry set off to his Aunt Pat's, who now lived with her fiancée in a two-bedroom flat in London. Terry was visibly distressed on arrival, and she invited him to lodge with them. When, on the following day, he returned to Peggy's house to pick up some belongings, he found John there. Seeing John, Terry felt an upsurge of rage, grabbed his jacket lapels and shoved him against the wall. He told Pat that 'I had wanted this moment to come. I said I was going to pay him back for the way he had treated me all those years. But he was terrified, shaking like a leaf, and I felt sorry for him. I thought to myself, "is this the man I've hated all these years?" I thought to myself "I can't be bothered, he's nothing", and I walked out.'

Based at Pat's, he managed to get his job back as an accounts clerk at the publishing company. There he befriended Bill Berks, a big-hearted, powerful union official who was to do his best to help Terry for several years. Along with his wife Mad (short for Madeleine), Bill ensured Terry got well-paid work, and he found him a flat in his parents' house. Terry developed an interest in politics: he read the left-wing magazine *New Statesman* and often contributed volubly at union meetings. He wore slick suits and a tie, and Mad recalled how alluring he looked. 'He was lovely. He had black hair, blue eyes, gorgeous teeth, he was about six feet tall, a handsome man.' He was delighted when she helped him furnish and stock his new flat, clasping simple utensils to his chest, telling her 'these are mine'.

The Berkses provided him with the nearest thing he had ever had to the familial warmth and responsiveness that had been completely absent from his main carers throughout his life. Mad got to know Terry well. She was puzzled why such a handsome man went with prostitutes on forays into Soho, but Terry explained that 'he couldn't afford the luxury of falling in love'. She subsequently discovered what he meant by this: he had realised he was someone who was so desperate to be cared for that he could not take the risk of depending on someone who might let him down.

When Mad had a baby, Terry had to sleep on their sofa. Mad found some blankets and chucked them to him. He lay down on the sofa and said, 'go on, tuck me in'. Mad commented, 'he just wanted me to tuck him in like a mum, although I was only two years older than him. So I stood there and tucked him in, and he went to sleep.'

Terry also showed Mad a battered photograph he kept in his wallet. It was of Jack Rosemberg, his biological father. He longed for the identity that the picture could confer and for the absent parent who had wanted him.

Living only three miles from Bromley, Terry started hanging out with Bowie again. He took the young teenager to visit Soho, including the jazz clubs. He also introduced Bowie to contemporary literary writers, like Jack Kerouac. The tales of alienated youth appealed to both of them. It was Terry who found Bowie a teacher who would teach him to play an alto saxophone that John had bought him. There was a powerful mutual admiration between the cool, relatively worldly-wise older brother and the younger one, hungry for new experience and full of imagination.

Sadly, the period of stability that had followed Terry's return from National Service ended in 1962, when Bill and Mad, who now had a second baby, decided to move to Falmouth, in Cornwall. They subtly indicated that there would be less time for Terry as their family grew, but he still followed them when the summer came. With two small children to care for, Mad could no longer tuck Terry in.

His mother remained as aloof as ever. Before the move to Cornwall, Peggy had made a rare phone call to Mad to hear how Terry was; she bemoaned the fact that he never contacted her but then showed why he did not: her lack of empathy towards him. 'He's a boy with a chip on his shoulder', she told Mad. She showed no sign of understanding that, not only had she been largely cold towards him, giving him no sense that he had a safe and loving home to go to, but her husband had been downright hostile.

In Falmouth, Terry took a series of jobs in pubs and hotels. No longer able to hang out with Bill and Mad, he teamed up with a pal and embarked on a summer of one-night stands. Terry was a successful lothario, humorous as well as good-looking. His conquests included a cub mistress, whom he lured out onto a Cornish hillside. Yet he still fought shy of any commitments, reputedly breaking the heart of another girl when he ended their relationship before it had hardly begun. With winter approaching and the Berkses no less busy with their domestic lives, he berated them for their betrayal of Socialist principles in becoming so bourgeois. Penniless, he had to turn to his drinking buddy for the train fare back to London.

Pat was now married, but she put him up, and he found a job in a bakery. By 1965, with Terry now in his late twenties, she noticed a marked change in his character. Having been punctilious about his appearance, he was now sloppy and unconcerned. His moods were violent and furious. At first Pat had supposed he was going through an 'angry young man' phase, but she soon realised this was something else.

She treated him as a surrogate child, waiting for him to come home until late. This began to annoy her husband. Terry would sometimes return drunk, his clothes torn from fights. Unbeknownst to Pat, he had slid into depression. Some mornings he would pretend to set off to work but then sneak back home to bed, black in mood. He managed to keep himself afloat until the summer, but Pat's husband – now an enemy every bit as keen to get rid of him as his step-father had been – was openly saying that he should leave; it must have rung bells.

The temporary solution was a flight back to Falmouth, but yet again he met rejection. The Berkses were no more in a position to welcome him than they had been before. They were shocked at how grubby and dishevelled he looked. At a party they took him to, his behaviour was so loutish and unpleasantly arrogant that Mad left early. Terry followed her, and, feeling alarmed by his state of mind, she told him to go to bed. The following morning she found him in their sitting room, staring out of the window. He told her that the human race was worthless and expanded the thought: 'Not one of them is worth saving, not one of them. What are we here for, what's it all about? It's all a load of crap.' Of himself, he said, 'I've read Freud and I've read Jung, and I know exactly where I'm heading.' Asked if that meant a doss house, he commented darkly, 'Oh no, I've got my pride.' It is likely that suicidal ideas were on his mind.

A week later, he went back to Pat's house. The atmosphere with her husband was just as bad, but Terry made it through the autumn and into the beginning of 1966, until he was involved in a fight, which ended with a court appearance and a fine. Pat had had enough and told him to leave, which he did the following morning. When she rang to ask Peggy if she knew where he was, the latter replied with characteristic detachment, 'Terry's a man. He's old enough to stand on his own two feet.'

What happened during the ensuing twelve months is not known, but early in 1967 Terry returned to Pat's house. Strangers opened the door: Pat had moved. Terry went to see his mother in Bromley. He turned pale when, over a cup of tea, she told him that Pat and her husband had emigrated to Australia. Shocked and rejected, he left without a word.

He walked to some caves, a local tourist attraction and once the venue for a concert performed by Bowie early in his career. The doors to the caves were locked, the area deserted. He later recalled that 'I heard a voice saying to me, "Terry, Terry", and I looked up, and there was this great light and this beautiful figure of Christ looking down at me, and he said to me, "Terry, Terry, I've chosen you to go out into the world and do some work for me." He said, "I've picked you out." And the light of his face was so intense that I fell to the ground. I was on my stomach, resting on my hands, looking down, and when I looked around me, there was this big burning, a big ring of fire all around me, and the heat was intense, it was terrible, and then it all disappeared.' This incident was to be memorialised by Bowie in the line 'a crack in the sky and a hand pointing down at me' in his song 'Oh! You Pretty Things' on the *Hunky Dory* album.

When the hallucinations ended, Terry rambled about in the nearby countryside, eventually falling asleep under a hedge. He spent the next eight days living rough, begging or stealing food. Finally, he stumbled into a greengrocer's shop and asked for an orange. The police were called, and they took him to Peggy's house. With her usual insensitivity, she lectured him furiously about his dishevelled state, and he became irate.

There is a robust and extensive body of scientific literature proving that hostile and negative responses from parents to a person who has had a schizophrenic episode make it much more likely that they will have a further one. Known as 'expressed emotion', in which families respond to the patient with hostility or over-control, it triples the likelihood of a further episode*. Peggy's reaction to Terry's episodes perfectly fits with this. However, the evidence also suggests that the negativity and confusing care of expressed emotion precede schizophrenic episodes and are a cause of it. How John had treated Terry long before he became schizophrenic was likely to have been one of its causes, likewise Peggy's irascibility (and Margaret's)*. Emotional abuse, such as Terry endured, is the strongest predictor of psychosis.

There is considerable evidence that hallucinations are not meaningless. Patients who are poor or of low status are more likely to hear voices to whom they feel subordinate. Apart from the humiliation and rejection experienced in his family, at the point of his breakdown Terry had the low social status of a man with no job and poor prospects. Studies show that whether you become schizophrenic at all, and what form your symptoms take, reflect social background and circumstances.

A survey of two million Danish people found that the more of your childhood you had spent in urban environments, the greater the risk of schizophrenia*. In rural areas, symptoms like loss of interest in appearance and cleanliness were the most common, whereas in cities you were more likely to hear voices and fear persecution*. Poor people are about twice as likely as the rich to suffer from schizophrenia*. As long ago as 1939, American sociologists showed that the nearer you lived to the slums at the centre of Chicago and the poorer you were, the greater your risk*. That its rate varies considerably between social classes (it is twice as common among the poor) and between races tends to be dismissed by psychiatrists, yet it is three times more frequent in American Afro-Caribbeans and up to 16 times more common in children of West Indian immigrants to Britain*. This latter is almost certainly nothing to do with genes because relatives of immigrant schizophrenics from the same genetic stock who remain living in the West Indies do not have these elevated rates of illness – emigration and the response of the host nation to this minority cause the increased rate*. Non-white people living in white neighbourhoods are more likely to become ill than those living in non-white areas*. Alongside racism, there are other huge pressures on Afro-Caribbean parents, some leading to extended periods separated from their children. In one study, of 38 Afro-Caribbeans who had become ill, a third had, during their childhood, been separated for more than four years from their mothers and half from their fathers*. Psychiatrists also play down the uncomfortable fact that the illness tends to last much longer and to be more severe in rich, industrialised nations compared with poor, developing ones (as strong a proof that modern life is detrimental as you could hope to find). In fact, if you go mad in a developing nation, you are fully ten times less likely to have any recurrence of the illness*.

Unusually for that era, Bowie (who by this time spent all his time in London developing his career) was at home at the time of Terry's psychotic episode at the caves and his appearance at Peggy's home, and he witnessed the whole shouting match. However, as was Bowie's way in his family, he did not take sides, remaining detached, thereby reinforcing Terry's sense of rejection. According to the close friend with whom Bowie was staying in London at that time and to whom he immediately returned, he invented the curious fiction that Terry was a merchant seaman who had been twice round the world. Despite their many years of intimacy, he never told his friend that Terry suffered from mental illness. Blocking Terry out was his way of coping, but he must have been deeply distressed by the incident.

Fortunately, John was filled with guilt at his former maltreatment of Terry and apologised there and then for it. There was nothing he would not do for his stepson, but this nurturant attitude came far too late.

Terry stayed at the house during the period of his recovery, supported considerably by John. He continued to live there until John's premature death, two years later, in 1969. He had treatment from a local hospital, where he stayed during the week, spending weekends at home, feeling quite settled there. But after John's death he rapidly became unsettled, because Peggy was now his main carer and he had lost his main ally (ironically, the man who had been his principal enemy). Pat commented that after John's death, 'Terry deteriorated very quickly, he wasn't getting the same comfort any more.' She maintains that 'If John had lived, Terry would have been all right.' Before long, Peggy declared that she could not care for Terry, and he was admitted to the local mental hospital, Cane Hill.

This Victorian asylum on the crest of a sizeable hill near Croydon was the place that Terry and everyone in the area dreaded (later described in Bowie's song 'All The Madmen'). It was known that, once admitted, the chances of getting out again were slim. Local children and teenagers would threaten each other with the words, 'You'll be sent to kay nil.' Pat felt it had not been necessary for Terry to go there. 'He was getting stroppy with his mother, feeling she was starting to reject him. But I didn't think Terry was ill enough for Cane Hill. It was a depressing, old-fashioned hospital. The food was appalling, the inmates seemed to have given up hope. Terry thought the same. He would say to me, "Pat, I can't stay here".'

Given the conviction among many psychiatrists that the illness of schizophrenia is no different in kind from a bacterial infection or cancer, the main treatment was, and is, medication. Terry received no talking therapy throughout the course of his illness – a situation that is all too common still today. About one quarter of patients are not helped at all by drugs, and around 15% of schizophrenics eventually commit suicide*. Where the drugs do work, the decrease in symptoms is not great – only a 15–25% improvement; set against this are terrible side-effects, commonly hand tremors and other neurological problems, accompanied by a sense of disorientated emptiness*. Even if there are talking therapies provided, it is usually cognitive behavioural therapy, which explicitly rejects the idea that childhood trauma should be considered in understanding symptoms. The idea that what the patient is saying makes any kind of sense is actively discouraged in the training of nurses, and family members are encouraged by psychiatrists to regard the delusions as nonsense.

Although hospitalised, Terry was permitted to stay with family members. During this time, Bowie was living in a South London house, Haddon Hall. Angie, his girlfriend (and subsequently, wife, and mother to his son), seems to have been sympathetic to Terry and would invite him regularly to stay there, for up to four weeks at a time. Friends from this period remember Bowie as having been concerned about his brother, sometimes driving him home to Cane Hill after his stays. There were times when Terry would wander off, and Bowie had to find him. Friends recall Terry as a marginal, ghostly presence. Nonetheless, the brothers were close, and, as described in Chapter 1, Bowie was preoccupied with him to a considerable extent, as shown by several songs written before, during and after this period.

At Cane Hill, Terry was desperately unhappy. He refused to accept that he had 'an illness' and was reluctant to take the severely sedating drugs he was prescribed. Sometimes he would just wander out of the hospital and disappear. One afternoon, in early 1971, he discharged himself and set off to sleep rough for a fortnight, ending up on Pat's doorstep (who had now returned to England) in a disturbed state, dishevelled, his hair and clothes infested with lice and fleas.

She cleaned him up and cared for him for several days, returning him to Cane Hill. Before taking Terry back, however, she sought help from Bowie, but he was very absorbed at a critical stage in his career. He was prepared to offer only to pay for the cost of the minicab to the hospital. Outraged by this, Pat did not meet with Bowie again until Peggy's funeral in the year 2000. She felt that Bowie had rejected both Terry and his family past at that moment, although it is clear from the lyrics of his songs that both remained major preoccupations.

During the following year, Terry met Olga, a fellow patient at Cane Hill, at a patients' dance, and they spent all their time together. Although Pat did not consider Olga worthy of him, since she was plain to look at and sturdy of build, Terry was enchanted, saying he 'could sit and look at her beauty for hours'. They married in 1972 – on the same day that Bowie gave his first-ever live performance as Ziggy Stardust. Bowie was not at the wedding (he performed Ziggy Stardust twice on that day, in different locations), but Terry's friends Bill and Mad Berks drove there all the way from Cornwall.

Bill was appalled by how scruffy, overweight and unkempt Terry had become. Nonetheless, he felt Terry was 'immensely happy'. Berks believes he was sad that Bowie was not there and had shown no sign he knew of the marriage. Peggy was there, appalled by the event, telling Berks that 'this is all wrong'.

Terry and Olga moved into a one-room flat and settled into a life that was far preferable to that at Cane Hill. Pat remembers Terry liking to sit drinking tea and smoking cigarettes, listening to music and chatting, their cat snoozing beside him when he took his regular afternoon nap. In the whole of Terry's life, apart from his brief interlude with the Berkses ten years earlier, this was the only period of security and harmonious domestic intimacy.

Terry followed Bowie's career avidly, taking great pride in his stardom. He would telephone the record company and ask them to send him a copy of each new album (which they did). However, after 1972 he was not to see Bowie in person for ten years.

In 1976, Terry and Olga moved to a larger flat. Terry now began drinking. He would frequently not take his prescribed drugs and began disappearing from home for days on end. When he became violent and was drinking heavily, Olga suggested he return to Cane Hill. Finally, she lost hope and sought a divorce, winning a court order that banned him from the home. In 1981, he was readmitted to Cane Hill.

Devastated, he told Pat, 'I've lost everything.' A well-read, intelligent man, Terry was well aware of the danger of institutionalisation, of becoming dependent on the routine and identity of 'a patient'. Heavily medicated, he knew how quickly he might give up hope. With Olga gone and Peggy, as unengaged as ever, insisting that there was nothing she could do, the whole burden of inventing a Plan B fell on Pat. She could offer no alternative, as her husband was implacably opposed to offering Terry a home. This left Bowie as the only remaining person who could save him.

By 1981, Bowie was a megastar. In the early- to mid-1970s, he had largely lost contact with his mother, much to her disgruntlement. In 1976 she telephoned Charles Shaar Murray, a famous rock journalist on the *New Musical Express*. More accustomed to writing drug-assisted and florid prose about the musical merits of bands, Shaar Murray found himself breaking the news that Bowie's mother only wanted him to show 'a little care and sympathy'. She was upset that he never contacted him and felt he was in debt to his parents.

Bowie was incensed when the interview was published and taken up by the national newspapers, and he forbade her from speaking to the press again. He was careful thereafter to ensure she visited him in America or Switzerland (where he then lived), and as a result she became suddenly very proud of him. She would approach complete strangers and inform them, to their startlement, that she was Bowie's mother.

Terry had never lost his admiration for Bowie. Whenever he heard his songs on the radio in Cane Hill, he would proudly tell the other patients of their relationship. In despair, he fixed on Bowie as his salvation, telling Pat, 'he could get me out of here'. Feeling that Bowie could pay for him to go into a private nursing home, Pat wrote several letters to Bowie, but received no reply.

In the summer of 1982, in deep depression, Terry threw himself out of the second-floor window of the hospital. Surprisingly, the injuries were only a broken arm and leg, although the damage to the arm proved serious and permanent. For Pat, this was the last straw: she blamed Bowie. Emulating Peggy's example, she telephoned *The Sun* newspaper. She portrayed him as 'callous and uncaring', and it was 'time his fans knew the other side of David Bowie – and time he faced up to his responsibilities'.

Her intervention worked. Two weeks later, Bowie visited Terry in the hospital where he was recovering from the fall. He kissed him and gave gifts of a radio-cassette recorder, books and cigarettes. They chatted about their childhood, and, according to Terry, Bowie vowed to get him out of Cane Hill. Not having seen Bowie for ten years, Terry was ecstatic. To what extent Bowie had committed to getting Terry out of the hospital is unclear, but according to Pat, Terry was now hanging all his hopes on that. She recalled that 'David's visit meant everything to him. He spent the next few months waiting, waiting for the promise to be fulfilled. He kept saying "when is David going to do it?"'

For the next few years, Pat made a monthly visit, and they would often discuss his childhood. Terry would puzzle how it was that Bowie had become the star. Terry had sung in pubs and felt that he was just as good-looking, so why Bowie and not him? This issue had not escaped Bowie's attention either. Speaking in 1974 to his half-sister Kristina, whom Bowie grew close to in later life, a similar question arose: why had Terry gone mad and not he?

By 1984, Terry had come to realise that Bowie was never going to save him. He was dispirited and self-loathing. The fall from the window had withered his right arm, and he walked with a limp. He felt useless and unattractive. He found the constant ravings of his fellow-patients maddening. When Pat told him she knew what he was going through, he replied, 'No you don't, I'm in bloody hell.'

According to Terry, on the rare occasions that Peggy visited, she spoke only about Bowie. When Pat remonstrated with Peggy that she did not show sympathy for Terry's arm injury, there was a big argument. Peggy accused her of being 'over-emotional' and of having an 'unhealthy attitude' towards him.

The summer of 1984 lifted Terry's spirits briefly, through an affair with another patient, but she was discharged that autumn, and his mood plunged into total despair. He was upset that his mother never visited and told Pat that he was going to die in the hospital. When Peggy did finally visit, for the first time in seven months, on Terry's 47th birthday, she talked about Bowie and how he was going to help her buy a new flat. Terry asked 'What about me, Mum? When am I going to get out of here?' Peggy replied, 'That's David's business.'

Two days after Christmas in 1984, Terry walked to a nearby railway station. As a train approached, he lay across the rails. At the last minute, he pulled his body back between the rails, and the train passed safely over him. Returned to the hospital, he spent five days in a locked ward, lying on his bed in a dazed state, apparently unaware of his surroundings.

Pat wrote, saying she would come to see him as soon as she could; but on 16 January 1985, she lost that opportunity. Standing on the platform of the local station at midday, Terry stepped down onto the rails and looked briefly towards an express train that was about to pass through at 70 mph. Although there was 200 yards' warning and the driver braked, all eight carriages passed over the place where Terry had been standing.

About a dozen people attended the funeral, of whom only Pat and Peggy were family members. They sat on opposite sides of the crematorium chapel. Bowie felt that his attendance would only lead to a mass of unwelcome publicity for his family and himself. He sent a basket of pink and yellow roses and chrysanthemums, and a card, reading, 'You've seen more things than we could imagine but all these moments will be lost, like tears washed away by the rain. God bless you – David.'

Bowie's question to his cousin Kristina as to why Terry and not he had gone mad was, indeed, the critical one. The answer lay not in their genes, but in the different kind of childhood experiences they had had.

Terry's childhood was maddening, Bowie's less so. Bowie suffered considerable emotional neglect from Peggy and was exposed to distressing trauma within his family, but, because he was less damaged, he was able to create the personas through which he could survive and, eventually, flourish. Terry was not so fortunate. Their family politics killed Terry, but, as we shall see, they made Bowie into a star.

FOUR

The favourite son

In 2002, a book of mine entitled *They F*** You Up* was published. Its title came from the first line of Philip Larkin's poem, *This Be The Verse*, and as part of the work of publicising the book, I recited the whole of the poem live on BBC Radio on two occasions. Coincidentally or not, about a week later Bowie was being interviewed by Terry Wogan in a chat show on BBC television. 'They fuck you up, your mum and dad, don't they?', Bowie quipped. To increasingly nervous titters from the studio audience, he proceeded to recite the whole poem:

> They fuck you up, your mum and dad.
> They may not mean to, but they do.
> They fill you with the faults they had
> And add some extra, just for you.
>
> But they were fucked up in their turn
> By fools in old-style hats and coats,
> Who half the time were soppy-stern
> And half at one another's throats.
>
> Man hands on misery to man.
> It deepens like a coastal shelf.
> Get out as early as you can,
> And don't have any kids yourself.

Precisely how he felt that his parents had fucked him up, Bowie did not explain to Wogan. Nor did he ever supply in his public utterances any details of how they had cared for him. His only comments about his background relate to how madness ran in his family and his fear that it would be passed on to him.

It is, however, possible to make some informed guesses about the way that both his parents had related to him, based on the reports of others who had shared his home or witnessed his early years. A good deal is known about his family dynamics – the pushes and pulls that existed in the home where he was raised.

Bowie was born at 9 am on 8 January 1947, in Brixton, South London. His parents had moved there a year earlier, bringing with them several removal-vans'-worth of emotional baggage to the family's politics.

When, in 1945, John had first met Peggy in the café where she was working as a waitress, wearing a tight black dress and a white pinafore, she was still a trim, vivacious woman. Born in 1913, she was, unusually for that era, still unmarried. Now aged 32, she had had many boyfriends and, even more significantly, had already given birth to two illegitimate children. (Nor, as we have seen, was she the only one of her sisters to have done so: Philip Larkin's other famous contention – that 'sex began in 1963'– is certainly not supported by the example of the Burns girls.)

John had also lived a good deal. The house into which he and Peggy moved had been bought by him jointly with his first wife, Hilda. Born in 1912 in the north of England, John was the only son of a prosperous boot and shoe dealer. Both his parents had died while he was young, and John was raised by a relative and then sent to a boarding public-school. On leaving there, he had sought to launch a career as a show-business entrepreneur – a thwarted ambition that was to play a significant role in Bowie's aspirations.

John lacked the kind of exuberantly outgoing and manipulative personality that is essential for an impresario. As Hilda later described him, 'he was very taciturn, nothing made him laugh. You never saw his lips move and you never saw him smile.' She had married him mainly in the hope that he would make her a star, using some money he had inherited when he turned 21. This project failed, and John lost the money, forcing him to work as a porter for some time before, in 1935, obtaining a job at the Head Office of the children's charity Dr Barnardo's. He remained there for the rest of his career, becoming their first Head of Publicity. Meanwhile Hilda, her hopes dashed, took a job as an usherette in a cinema, and within a year their marriage was, effectively, over. During this time he had an affair that resulted in a daughter (Annette), whom Hilda generously adopted, even though John offered no support. They had remained firm friends.

John's time in the army in the Second World War 'humanised him', according to Hilda. Having previously been abstemious, he returned more extrovert, a drinker and smoker. When the war ended, John and Hilda used the pay saved from their wartime jobs to buy the house in Brixton as a future home for Annette. When John married Peggy, at first they lived in (the endlessly tolerant) Hilda's cramped flat. She was relieved when they moved into the Brixton house.

At the point when Peggy met John, she was on the lookout for a Steady Eddy with whom to have a family. Peggy felt that John was courteous and cultivated. After a long line of more or less 'unsuitable' lovers during the course of the war, she was pleased to be able to present a man in a smart tweed overcoat, collar turned up, neat cravat at his neck. Her parents – and especially her socially insecure mother, Margaret – approved of a public-school-educated gentleman.

A shadow was, however, cast upon the marriage by 'the only man I really loved' – Jack Rosemberg, Terry's father. John and Peggy's marriage was loveless, just as Peggy's parents' marriage had been.

Like any adults, they brought their upbringings with them to the Brixton house. A critical factor was the discomfort felt by both of Bowie's parents, especially Peggy, when it came to displaying emotion. A key witness to this was Peggy's youngest sister, Pat. According to her, Peggy liked newborns but, after that, 'when they get to a certain age, she can't communicate'. With Terry, 'I never saw her kiss him or put her arms round his shoulders, or touch him, nothing'; and this continued with Bowie. There was 'no hugging or kissing' by either parent, as Pat recalled.

Other witnesses have also spoken about this. A close friend of Bowie at primary school described the care Peggy supplied and the family atmosphere as follows: 'She'd feed him, clothe him, but there was no cuddling, nothing like that. She'd be sitting there reading. It was just as if he was there, but not there. There was no sign of affection at any time. I don't think it was a family. It was a lot of people who happened to be living under the same roof.' In his late teens, when Bowie brought a girlfriend (the singer Dana Gillespie) to visit his parents, her account was strikingly similar: 'I was in a house where he didn't love his parents like I loved mine . . . it didn't seem like a house with love in it.' Interestingly, years later, talking to a close intimate, Bowie confided that he could not remember anything about his childhood before the age of 8. Studies show that people who cannot remember early experiences are much more likely to have been emotionally neglected or maltreated*.

That neither John nor Peggy were very physically expressive and loving is not surprising, given their own experiences. John had lost his parents early and had been dispatched to boarding school. Such schools, while not quite as bestial as the nineteenth-century institution described in *Tom Brown's Schooldays*, were still very austere and allowed for a great deal of bullying in the 1920s, when John attended his. As a result, it would be normal for him to be somewhat emotionally frozen and closed up.

An even more important role was played by Peggy's mother, Margaret, and the way she had nurtured her children. Peggy's unease with loving displays was, evidently, intergenerational: her mother too was very averse to physical displays of affection. Taken overall, it is highly probable that both Peggy and her mother would have qualified for a diagnosis of personality disorder (self-focused, febrile, moody). There is good evidence that 85% of such mothers have difficulty in relating responsively and consistently to their babies when they are 1 year old*.

The transmission of cold mothering from Margaret to Peggy is consistent with the findings of studies on both humans and animals. Overall, the kind of early care a monkey receives precisely predicts the kind of adult and parent it will become and its brain chemistry*.

Compared with rhesus monkeys reared by their mothers, those separated from their mothers at birth and reared until the age of 6 months only with their peers, without an alternative parent, are more easily frightened of strangers and of unfamiliar experiences. They slide to the bottom of monkey-status hierarchies, whereas the more secure, socially assured, mother-reared monkeys are at the top.

Less extreme variations in early care, however, also have similarly large effects: monkey infants separated from their mothers only briefly and occasionally during the first 14 weeks of life are just as insecure as are those reared totally apart from their mothers. Tested at age 4 years, they still show evidence of depleted brain chemicals.

Above all, patterns of mothering are passed down from mother to daughter. The amount of contact with the mother precisely predicts the amount that she bestows on her own child. When those reared by their peers become mothers themselves, they are significantly more neglectful or abusive of their offspring than are those who had been mother-reared, repeating the cycle of deprivation.

The same is found in rats: the more a mother had been licked as a pup, the more she licks her own offspring.

The similarity in mothering across generations might be simply a genetic inheritance, but this has been disproved. The amount of contact with the particular monkey daughter has been compared with the mother's average *for all her daughters*. A daughter's subsequent mothering reflects her particular experience, rather than the average for all her sisters. Rather than being a genetic tendency inherited from the mother, the unique care the daughter has received determines the subsequent pattern of mothering.

Another theory is that a genetically difficult baby could make the mother uncaring. This was contradicted by a study of what are called 'highly reactive' infant monkeys – those that are very difficult to care for because they over-react to the slightest sound or movement, probably as a result of problems during the pregnancy or birth. They were fostered out to either average mothers or exceptionally nurturing ones. The exceptionally nurtured young monkeys grew up even more socially well-adjusted than normal infants fostered by average mothers. Nurture was so influential, in other words, that it could turn a difficult infant into a superior adult. Furthermore, when the generation of offspring in the study grew up and themselves had infants, their parenting style, whether exceptionally nurturing or average, precisely mirrored the kind of care they had received as infants, regardless of whether their original infant personality had been highly reactive or not. This could be taken to suggest that, had Peggy been passed at birth to a warmer, more nurturing mother than Margaret, she would have been more like that herself with Terry and Bowie.

Much of what goes for monkeys seems to go for humans*. It is a simple but important point: babies and toddlers need consistent, loving care if they are to grow up secure and mentally healthy and to become nurturant parents themselves. A study of over 1,700 maltreated children showed the crucial role of early nurture*. The children in the sample were chosen specifically because they were likely to be impaired and therefore difficult to care for. Measured as infants, 85% of them were neurologically impaired and at high risk of behaviour problems and language deficits. However, follow-up at the ages of 18 months and 3 years shows that the more the children's maternal or other nurture had improved, the greater was the likelihood that they were overcoming their initial impairment. For at least a decade the myth has been doing the rounds that it is babies' temperaments that determine the care they receive, not vice versa. However, this study was able to show quite clearly that it was the environment in which the babies had been reared that was crucial in determining the outcome.

The evidence shows, above all, that there is a strong tendency for mothers to care for their infants in ways similar to the way they had been nurtured. For example, in a study of 180 mothers, 70% of those who had themselves been abused as children either maltreated their own children or provided inadequate care*. Of the mothers who had not been maltreated as children, only one provided inadequate or maltreating care. At age 18, 90% of the maltreated children qualified for diagnosis with at least one psychiatric illness. By contrast, only one of the children who had had good care from their mothers qualified. This is strong evidence that man hands on misery to man, as Philip Larkin put it – and that man hands on emotional health, as well*.

Humans and monkeys do, of course, differ in important respects. We have complex language, which enables us to use concepts, creating self-consciousness; because of this we are far more able than monkeys to control both our environment and ourselves. As parents, we can choose to care for our children differently from the way we were nurtured. While, overall, humans do tend to follow the pattern that had been imposed on them, a proportion decide to do the opposite or to create a pattern that is different from the one they experienced, in a way that is neither a repetition nor a reaction against what went before. For example, in the study of 180 mothers, in the case of those who had been abused but did not go on to maltreat their children there had usually been mitigating factors, such as having had love from another relative*.

As for Peggy, she did repeat to a great extent the care she had received from Margaret. They shared a lack of warmth and a dislike of hugging and displays of affection, along with a desire to keep up appearances. Pat recalls that 'David was always clean and tidy and spotless – my sister made a thing of that. Every five minutes she would say "pull your sock up", "have you washed your face?"' Consequently, both Bowie and Terry were always particular about how their clothing and their hair might look to others.

At the age of 6, Bowie was something of a good-goody: a demure child with a neat side-parting and a ready smile, who sang in the school choir and was a member of the local cub-scout troop. Pat recalled that 'He had beautiful blue eyes and lovely blond hair. He always liked to comb it his way, forward, with a quiff by his ear. If you combed it he always had to do it again himself. He looked at himself a lot in the mirror. He was a vain child and he always liked to look different.' Bowie's preoccupation with his appearance and his capacity to make himself so visually alluring and fascinating was something he had learnt from Peggy.

There is a likelihood that, insofar as Peggy engaged with Bowie (or Terry) at all, it was to be controlling. Her children mattered to her mainly as potential vehicles for humiliation in the eyes of neighbours and family, or else as potential sources of pride, if she could bask in the reflected glory of their successes: when Bowie became a superstar, Peggy bitterly resented his lack of contact with her, and she forced him to let her share in his fame.

There is a mass of evidence that over-control by parents can be maddening and, especially, depressing to children*. Over-control entails obsessively fussing over tiny details of children's behaviour, such as the way they eat or play or work. This removes a sense of agency from the children and teaches them to feel helpless, interfering with the development of individuality and increasing the risk of feeling without an identity and disconnected from reality. A recent study that compared Italian and English parents found much higher levels of over-control on the part of the Italians*. However, this did not result in disturbance in the offspring, as long as it was combined with warmth. As many of the Italian parents were very affectionate, there was no difference overall between the two nations in the amount of distress in the children of over-controlling parents. The greater warmth cancelled out the greater over-control.

In Bowie's case, although neither parent was physically demonstrative, the damaging combination of over-control and lack of warmth may have been reduced by his critical status in the family: he was very much the favoured child, especially for John. We shall see that this was the critical factor that enabled Bowie to become a star.

Bowie was by no means the only child in his home. Off and on, he shared it with Terry, with his cousin Kristina (for two periods when Una was too disturbed to look after her) and, briefly, with Annette (John's daughter by Hilda, his first wife). As we saw in chapter 4, Annette recalled that Bowie was 'the be-all and end-all – he was the god of the house'. They owned a television, which was unusual in that era, and even when he was small, it was David who decided what they watched. (Not that the choice was great: just the two BBC channels.) As a young child, he always wanted to see *The Flowerpot Men*, and when older, the science-fiction series, *The Quatermass Experiment*.

His father, John, for whom Bowie felt the greatest love (in adult life he was to wear and treasure a crucifix he had given him), often bought him exciting presents, including his first saxophone. John also encouraged him to be enterprising. In 1962, at the age of 15, Bowie wrote to the US Embassy asking for information about the baseball World Series and American football players and teams. To his surprise, they responded by sending him a full American football outfit, including a helmet, and a photographer came along to record his interest. Using it as a publicity stunt, they sent out a press release captioning the photograph of him dressed in the kit with 'Limey Kid Digs Yank Football'.

When Bowie was 6, John became Head of Publicity at Barnardo's. Until then, the charity had eschewed media attention, but for John this was a chance to fulfil his impresario longings. He staged charity concerts, basking in the company of stars backstage. Whenever possible, he would take Bowie to these events, including one in 1956, where the pop star Tommy Steele performed. Afterwards, Kristina overheard John tell Steele that his son 'had aspirations to be a performer'. John gave Bowie an autograph book, which he assiduously filled with famous names. According to Kristina (to whom Bowie grew close in the 1970s, when she was a theatrical agent in New York), 'Uncle John wanted him to be a star'. Indeed, throughout the long period while Bowie struggled to become successful, John provided practical assistance in obtaining publicity. He also taught Bowie the rudiments of how to sell himself, helping to make him a supremely talented self-publicist.

But being the favourite child also had its downsides, one being that it inspired considerable aggression, to the point of abuse, on the part of Kristina. She was 2 in 1944 when her mother, Una, suffered her first schizophrenic breakdown. When she was 4, she and her mother moved in with John and Peggy. Una was largely incapable of caring for Kristina – for example, Peggy would find Kristina freezing because Una had placed her on top of the blankets instead of underneath them. The arrival of baby Bowie, in January 1947, was not welcomed by Kristina.

She remembers smearing excrement from his nappies on the wall, pretending that he had done it. When Una had to be hospitalised in the autumn of that year, Kristina was left with John and Peggy. Her aggression against Bowie now worsened: she punched him to make him cry and his first steps were greeted with howls of laughter, then she shoved him back to the floor. 'I intended to be the only one who walked', she later recalled. Peggy and John decided that Kristina would have to live elsewhere.

Kristina began a hideous five-year period of being shunted from care homes to foster parents, when not with her severely distressed mother. In 1953, when she was 11, she was placed with foster parents only a quarter of a mile from Bowie's home, in the hope that Peggy might eventually take her back into the family.

Kristina started spending as much time as she could at the now 7-year-old Bowie's house. Like many institutional- ised children who have been fostered*, her academic abilities flourished with the help of middle-class, educated parenting, and she gained a place in the local grammar school. She was, however, still emotionally distressed as a result of the earlier neglect and maltreatment. She describes Bowie's home as 'the only family that I ever knew', and she hoped that his parents would let her live with them permanently, rather than staying with the foster parents.

The trouble was that Bowie was the favoured child, and Kristina still felt very envious of that. She recalled that he was 'polite and well-bred – he adored me and followed me around'. What annoyed her was the constant flow of toys. 'Every time I went there, David would say, "look at my new gramophone" . . . he used to infuriate me because we would go somewhere and I'd see something I liked and I'd say "can I have that?" and they'd say "no, pipe down". David would stand there and say, "that's so nice, may I touch it if I'm very care- ful?" and they'd let him touch it and end up giving it to him.'

She would punch him and find other cruel ways to get her own back. When she told Bowie that if he held his guinea pigs up by their tails, their eyes would fall out, 'he cried bit- terly. He was very naïve and trusting as a little child.' After two years, her foster parents gave up on her, and she was found new ones far away, in Dorset.

The other problem for Bowie was that the favouritism made him feel guilty about Terry. Kristina recalled that 'he [Bowie] felt very responsible, as children do, for the fact that he was the favourite child because of his father, and he was given attention by his father and Terry wasn't'. The relationship with Terry mattered so much to Bowie because he was the only person in the household to whom he felt physically close. During Bowie's early life and his teens, Terry was also a vital stimulus for Bowie's imagination. They played exciting games, and he was a key source of playfulness in the household. Kristina recalls him as a lively storyteller, an inspiration for Bowie's subsequent capacity for pretence. But witnessing his parents' hostility and coldness towards Terry and the latter's consequent distress led, she believes, to Bowie learning to suppress signs of emotion and developing a protective shell. In addition, what with the lack of early affection on the part of his mother and the abusive periods with Kristina, Bowie may have felt the situation so distressing that he 'dissociated' from it.

Dissociation, a key symptom of personality disorder, is feeling at one remove from oneself and from one's environment; it is a way of coping. It can provide the detachment necessary to achieve feats of intellectual or artistic excellence; but it can also lead to emotional remoteness from others, a lack of commitment. In later life, Bowie's physical beauty was combined with a superficial charm that enabled him to skate from relationship to relationship, both professional and personal. He would give himself to a person or a band of musicians, seem to fully commit, but then, always holding his deeper self back, be able to disconnect as if the relationships had never existed. It may have left him isolated and remote, but it enabled him to slide between musical genres and between professional and sexual relationships without a care and with extraordinary adeptness.

The potential for Bowie to be dissociated probably had its roots in the early care he received from Peggy. Personality disorder entails a weak sense of identity (self), febrile moods and a feeling of unreality*. About half of men and one third of women who, as children, had been placed in institutions because their parents were unable to cope suffer from personality disorders. One study followed such children into adult life and found that of the many traumas that had happened to them, one stood out: disrupted parenting before the age of 2*. The definitive study followed a large sample of infants through to the age of 18*. If the care before age 2 had been neglectful or abusive or disharmonious, the infant was at greater risk of dissociation at age 18. The children were observed all the way through, and so it was possible to show that maltreatment (including physical and sexual abuse) after the age of 2 did not increase the risk of dissociation at the age of 19 as much. Moreover, good early care reduced the risk if traumatisation happened after the age of 2.

Another study, with very similar findings, also followed a sample of high-risk infants from birth through to age 19*. The quality of maternal care during the first 18 months was carefully measured in a laboratory setting and at home. At home, the lack of positive interaction with the baby (such as engaging in peek-a-boo games or responding to the infant's cries) and flatness of emotion (such as an impassive face or a torpid, unemotional state) were strongly associated with dissociation at age 19. In the laboratory, the infants were more likely to be dissociated at age 19 if there had been disrupted communication from the mother – such as inappropriate responses to clear infant cues (e.g. smiling when the infant looked sad), backing away from the infant when it greeted her and self-focused behaviour when the infant needed her (e.g. saying 'Mummy needs to brush her hair'). Overall, half of the reason that the 19-year-olds were dissociated was explained by care before the age of 18 months.

It seems highly probable that when they were small, neither Bowie nor Terry had very responsive, empathic and consistent care from Peggy. Unfortunately, if a mother is unresponsive early on, she tends to remain so throughout her offspring's childhood*, although there are some parents who react better to babies than to toddlers, or to older children than to younger. In Terry's case, from the age of 6 months, he was looked after by Margaret, who had produced three psychotic daughters. Such inadequate early care created a vulnerability to what are known as schizophrenic-spectrum problems in both Terry and Bowie (as indicated by the presence of dissociation), the potential for a weak grip on reality and a lack of a sense of who they were (of identity or sense of self), with Terry's exposure to Margaret's coldness putting him at even greater risk. There is good evidence linking unresponsive early care to adult schizoid-spectrum disorders*. On top of that, because of their family's politics, they received different care subsequently, while growing up.

In Bowie's case, his mother's cold, physically unresponsive care may explain why he could be like that himself in later life. At the height of his fame, he seems to have developed a horror of being touched by strangers. It may also help to explain his fear of dependence, for he became a man frightened of falling in love. Before his forties, it only happened once, and that was enough for Bowie. Such discomfort with dependence and with physical proximity are common in the personality-disordered*.

As a toddler, he was also punched and mocked and physically abused by his cousin Kristina. This happened again to him intermittently between the ages of 7 and 9, when she spent a good deal of time at his home. Childhood physical abuse is found in the histories of about two thirds of personality-disordered adults*. This could have created dissociation, as might have witnessing the maltreatment of his brother*.

Bowie's mother was over-controlling, fussily insisting on an exaggerated concern with his appearance. This, in itself, is a predictor of personality disorder*.

The favouritism he was given by both his parents, but especially his father, was complicated by the feelings of guilt it aroused about Terry. Even more, it may have given Bowie a strong sense of entitlement and an exaggerated self-esteem. This difference in what is called ego-resiliency may have kept him on the right side – the personality disorder side – of the madness line. A study of maltreated and non-maltreated children has shown that the earlier and the more severe the maltreatment, the worse the outcome*.

Bowie had many years during which he must have secretly doubted if he would succeed – yet to others he seemed supremely self-confident. A member of a 1963 band he was in recalled that 'David showed more or less total commitment. Of all of us, he had the most positive view of becoming successful. He had no doubts that he was going to do it, no doubts at all.' His manager of that time, Ken Pitt, remembered that 'He had natural charisma. He walked around like a star . . . he had that quality, that star quality, right from the very first minute I met him. David believed in himself absolutely and he was prepared to work very hard for success.' Bowie never seemed to let the failures get him down for long. Between 1964 and 1969, there was a succession of bands, managers, recording contracts and failed singles; it was not until 1973 that he became a superstar.

As his songs often displayed, he wrestled with both exaggerated self-love (perhaps there was a joking reference to this in one the songs released just two days before he died, '★Blackstar': 'I'm the great I am') and self-loathing. His parents accorded him a special status, but largely through allowing him a privileged position in the family hierarchy, as indicated by material possessions, not through direct affection. To others he displayed an unshakeable confidence in his power to persuade and charm, a sense of entitlement to greatness. But a solid sense of self-efficacy comes from having felt loved, not from being favoured. Deep down, Bowie may have felt like a fraud, in danger of being found out, an impostor. This feeling is common in people whose parents put pressure on their children to succeed and be perfectionists*, as John undoubtedly had done. John had contacts in the media and was, on a few occasions, able to use them to promote his son – for example, he obtained a plug in London's *Evening Standard* for one of Bowie's early songs. John taught him how publicity worked, and in his teens Bowie was already highly skilled at creating publicity scams, seeking out managers who also liked to play that game. In 1964, when Bowie was only 17, the newspapers were full for a week of a cooked-up story about how Bowie had been banned from appearing on a programme because of his long hair. To exploit this, Bowie invented a *League for the Protection of Animal Filaments* and, as its self-appointed spokesman, pronounced his indignation at the persecution of the long-haired during a 90-second interview on the BBC TV programme *Tonight With Cliff Michelmore*. This was not Bowie's only TV coverage in that year. His single 'Liza Jane' was blagged by his manager onto the prime time *Juke Box Jury* (it was also given coverage on *Ready, Steady Go* and *The Beat Room*). The format was that four panellists would predict whether a disc was going to be a Hit or a Miss. Presciently, three of the panellists predicted a Miss (the comedian Charlie Drake was the one dissenter).

John described 'Liza Jane' as 'awful, just terrible' to his newspaper contact, suggesting that he had high standards and was not a soft-headed, indulgent father. Indeed, it may be that Bowie's work ethic and capacity for application came in part from exposure to John's healthy perfectionism and scepticism, combined with Peggy's insistence on Bowie being well turned-out and organised. It was a great sadness to Bowie that his father died at just the point when he did finally break through, with his song 'Space Oddity', in 1969.

But such pressure to succeed may have created narcissistic (exaggerated self-love) and omnipotent (fantasies of being able to achieve anything) defences*. The weak sense of self and weak grip on reality resulting from his early care would have boosted his vulnerability to such illusions. They are common in people with personality disorder*.

Having failed his 11-plus, Bowie left school at 15 with a single O-level. The school's final verdict on him was that he was 'a complete exhibitionist – if he was capable of continuous effort his ability would have been put to better use'. His outwardly supreme confidence was certainly not based on any recognised academic achievements. His sense of imposture must have been powerful and is strongly associated with personality disorder*. However, interestingly, both his narcissism and his omnipotence will have played a crucial role in enabling him to power on through all the adversities on his way to stardom. While strongly linked to personality disorder, narcissism and omnipotence are also linked to success, especially in teenagers*.

Bowie had times of substance abuse: in the late 1960s he had periods of heavy marijuana use, and in the mid-1970s he abused cocaine for several years. At least until his forties, he was also addicted to casual sexual encounters. Substance abuse and personality disorder are closely related, the latter causing the former, in most cases*. Personality disorder and compulsive sexual behaviour also go together*.

If Bowie had been assessed by a psychiatrist during his late teens and early forties, he would probably have been identified as someone with personality disorder, on the schizophrenic spectrum, although (except during his cocaine period) not deluded, as Terry was. Most telling of all, he was often reported to have an air of detachment about him, of dissociation. This capacity to step back from any situation may have saved him from self-destruction during his rise to stardom. But it was a strong indication of personality disorder*.

There are countless substance-abusing, personality-disordered people with artistic leanings or with a sense that they have special gifts that will eventually lead to public recognition. What makes Bowie's story so important is the way he managed both to realise his ambitions and to express his emotional turmoil by creating musical personas. This was possible for him because of the way the universal capacity for pretence had developed in his particular case.

FIVE

From children's play
to madness

The boundary between real and pretend was shakier in Terry than in Bowie. This may have been primarily because as a small child Terry had been cared for by Margaret, a woman whose nurturing had already resulted in the raising of three psychotic daughters. But there was also another important difference. Bowie, the favoured son, had had a strong impetus to enjoy personas, like his father's picture of him as a future pop star; his self-admiration and playfulness were nurtured. He had the companionship of Terry to enliven his early years. Terry, on the other hand, had had no such figure and none of these advantages.

Before turning to the consequences for Bowie's artistic work in the next two chapters, I will briefly explain how childhood experience of the real and pretend reflects the care a child receives. If a proper demarcation is drawn between real and pretend, sanity prevails; if, on the other hand, the distinction is unclear during childhood, then this puts the adult subsequently at risk of delusional states. Understanding all this may provide some of the clues to Bowie's ability to find sanity through art and to Terry's slide into delusion.

REAL AND PRETEND IN CHILDREN'S PLAY

By around 2 years of age, nearly all children can engage in pretence, mostly expressed through play. American 2-year-olds spend between 5% and 20% of their time in fantasy play. Not only do they play pretend games from a remarkably young age, but they can also recognise when others do so*. Several classic experiments have proven this.

In one, children observe an experimenter pretend to fill two cups with imaginary water from a jug and then drink the imaginary liquid from only one of the cups. The child is then invited to take a drink from one of the cups. From 18 months onwards, the child is increasingly likely to choose the cup from which the experimenter drank, with the majority doing so by age 2 years. There is no real water in either cup, yet the children are able to act as if the cup that the experimenter drank from did have water in it. That children do this proves that they are capable of pretence from around the time they first acquire language. (By age 18 months, on average, they are capable of two-word utterances, like 'mama: milk!'.) But it also proves that they are able to understand that others can pretend. Since the experimenter drank from a cup without any real water, the children have grasped that the experimenter was also pretending.

A similar classic example is where a mother or experimenter picks up a banana and uses it as if it were a telephone. The child quickly understands the gag and does the same, speaking into the banana–telephone. The child could only do this if it can pretend. Because the child realises that the banana is symbolising a telephone rather than actually being one, it can engage in the illusion. The child can also only do this if it also grasps that the adult is pretending.

Pretence becomes more possible, the more a child is able

to untangle who it is from others. When followed from the age of 15 to 24 months, the more a toddler uses first-person pronouns ('I', 'me'), indicating it has a concept of the difference between 'me' and 'you', the greater the likelihood that it will be able to engage in pretend play. Likewise, the more a toddler can recognise itself in a mirror, the more pretend play. Separating emotionally from parents also entails separating what is real from the pretend.

There has to be a way for the child to indicate to itself that the banana is a pretend telephone, or that the cup contains only imaginary water. Otherwise, the child is going to start treating empty cups as full ones, or picking up bananas imagining they can really be used to speak with and hear others.

Adults use various signals to convey that they are in pretend mode, which is different from the everyday: they might stop the cup a few inches from the lips, or make ostentatious slurping noises or exaggerated facial expressions, like a big smile, conveying that the usual rules of reality do not apply here. The child realises that this is 'as-if' drinking or phoning, rather than actual.

The imaginary and the real must not contaminate each other. Without a quarantine, children would become hopelessly confused. They create a separate box, or a place in their minds – a zone where the normal rules are suspended, where almost anything can happen, much like what occurs during dreams.

All of this happens intuitively. It is impossible to explain the principles of play to a young toddler, nor do parents normally try: the ability to play must be inborn. When we engage in peek-a-boo with a baby, it is enjoying the surprise of 'now you see it, now you don't'. We do not explain what is going on. Likewise, with toddlers, if you invent a scenario involving imaginary phones, they automatically 'get' it.

From around the age of 3 years, children can live for extended periods in the imaginary space of pretend. For example, a 4-year-old girl I know liked to be taken out to ride on a pony. Somewhat puzzlingly, she also preferred it if the owner and her daughter remained outside the field when she was riding. It emerged that she liked to imagine that her riding was being filmed for a children's television programme, in which she was quite certain she would be starring. Such beliefs are both close to delusions and yet quite distinct from them: they are temporary illusions achieved by using the pretend experiential box. The girl knows perfectly well that when out of it and back in the real box, no such programme is being made; she is not actually deluded.

This same little girl explained to her parents that she was starring in her school nativity play. She insisted that she had many lines in the play and that both parents must attend to witness her performance. As the date approached, the parents were worried, because the girl had not been supplied with the script. All was revealed when her teacher explained that the girl was not playing the lead part. (In fact, when they turned up on the day, she was barely visible on stage.) They tactfully did nothing to disabuse the girl of her pretend role, who was completely untroubled by the conflict between what she had told her parents and the reality, although she would certainly have understood the truth of the matter. They realised she could distinguish pretend from real, but they wanted her to continue enjoying her illusions (rather than delusions) of grandeur.

If the walls between pretend and real experiential boxes break down, illusion becomes delusion. Little girls or adults who believe they are starring in a show or a television programme when they are not, and still continue to believe this after the reality has been demonstrated to them, are suffering from a delusion. The collapse of the lines of demarcation between the pretend and the real is one way to characterise madness.

Young children can shift effortlessly between imaginary scenarios and convert the identity of objects accordingly. A stick can move from being a sword to being a laser gun and back to a stick as a child switches between contexts, such as being a knight in battle with another boy, superhero in a game with another, to poking a drain when asked to help daddy unblock it. These transitions might take place within a period of five minutes without any sense of disjunction.

This is the precursor of the multiple selves that adults take for granted and effortlessly enact. We, too, might take a phone call from a boss who is dissatisfied with a piece of work we have done, making us downcast, then smile at our child as we applaud her for finishing her homework, then look lasciviously at our partner as he returns home from work, all within five minutes. With no sense of self-contradiction, we move smoothly between personas and roles, and accompanying emotions, each with its own narrative history that is personal to the individual with whom we are communicating, finding appropriate words and gestures relevant to the scripting of the different dramas. Pretences and play oil the wheels of the transitions.

The essence of play is a flexibility about what is real. The literal gives way to a more variable universe in which words or actions can mean something different from normal. The real may be exaggerated (extra loud instructions or laughs) or truncated (just one word used to signify a complex sequence of gestures). A playful nip can signify a bite, a growl can indicate the presence of a mighty lion. In play, there is always an element of amusement and a sense of fun, even if something tragic is being enacted. It is primarily self-motivated – not to please others, but for its own sake, rather than for a reward or in search of praise.

Play is at its purest around the ages of 3 to 5 years, but it lasts well into middle childhood. Aged 8, my son took to making high squeaking noises; he told me he was Nibbles The Squirrel. At such times I was Mr Huggles. While hardly under any great pressure at school, he was having to get his head around being able to write legibly and similar demands, to conform to the adult external world. As a reasonably talented soccer player, he was doing weekly training with a top Premiership soccer club – an unfamiliar weekly experience of needing to be on his best behaviour and to perform to high standards if he was to be kept on. Although done for pleasure, Nibbles proved a useful persona when dealing with situations in which he felt such pressures, or to help him forget about them. For example, at the end of a long day, I mistakenly suggested to him that he do some handwriting practice, and he replied, 'I'm going into Nibbles mode now, Dadda.' Hopping off squeaking, he proceeded to pick up a small policeman and astronaut from his Lego table and passed a peaceful half-hour banging them together with 'boom' and 'bang' noises. On another occasion, out on the golf course, tired and probably fed up with my exhortations to keep a straight left arm, he struck up a conversation with his 'friends': some real squirrels in nearby trees.

On returning from school one day, having been bullied by some older boys, he told me how lucky he felt he was to have suffered such maltreatment. Puzzled, I asked why, and he replied (speaking slowly, as if I was half-witted), 'Well, Dadda, I love my life. If I could live all my life like as a happy little elf, jumping up and down, like a Nibbles, playing with squirrels and rabbits all the time, I would get a horrid shock when people were horrid to me.'

Like most parents, I am constantly amazed by the richness of children's' imaginations. At one time, while we were out in the car, my son suddenly burst out laughing. 'Imagine Lord Voldemort's birthday party! Harry Potter would have to join in the singing, they would all be singing 'Happy birthday to you, happy birthday to you, happy birthday Dear Voldemort, happy birthday to you!' On another occasion, he said, 'When I was younger, I asked Father Christmas for a real helicopter, and I thought it would really really land in our garden. But now I realise that he has about 8,000 elves working for him, so he is probably broke, so he couldn't give me a helicopter.' (This was, needless to say, a period when we were a bit hard up, and he was aware of the fact.) Luckily for us, financial problems do not cast a pall over our family, but he has said to me, 'Don't worry about money, Dadda. When I am a Premiership player, I will give you a million pounds.'

As children age, they playfully explore what is real and what is not, with increasing sophistication. Both my children (we have a 14-year-old daughter as well as our son, who is now 11) went through a period of asking 'why?' – on an infinite loop. Why are children born? Because they have grown big enough to come out of Mummy's tummy. But why are they big enough? Because over the nine months since they existed, they get bigger. But why do they get bigger over those nine months? And so on, and so on, *ad nauseam*. From around the age of 7, my daughter occasionally attended talks I gave at literary festivals, and she developed a longing to be given the chance during the Q&A section to ask a question. Because she knew I did not know the answer, her question was to be 'Why is the sky blue?'

At age 9, my son enjoyed perplexing people with 'If you could take a drug which meant you would live forever, would you take it?' He vexed me with finely judged alternatives to vexing possibilities: 'If you could have only one box set, would it be: *Modern Family* or *The Simpsons*?', or, 'If you had to get rid of a player, which would it be: Mikel or Torres?' (two equally disastrous members of the Chelsea soccer team that we support). His killer was 'If you had to write *nice* things about one of them, would it be: Margaret Thatcher or Richard Dawkins?' (two of my *bêtes noires*). I am sure your children come up with similar gags. Like most children of his age, he is constantly questioning why the *status quo* exists, what is real, and why it is so, with questions like 'If adults can drink alcohol and they get drunk, why can't children?' – not as easy to answer as it might seem – or the assertion, 'I go to my office [i.e. school] every day, why don't I get paid for it?'

Pretence and playfulness are encouraged more in some families and in some children within the family, and in some societies, and less in others. The more a parent plays with a child, the more the child plays overall. The more fantastical the play with the parent, the more fantasy in the child's play in other contexts. A survey of 16 nations found that mothers from Britain, the United States and Ireland reported over twice as much imaginative play among their children than did those in other countries*. In those three countries, over half of mothers reported imaginative play; in China, however, it was 19%, and in Vietnam only 5%.

When playing, the themes and forms also vary across cultures. Anglo-Saxon children are more prone to fantasy, emphasising dangerous or exciting alternative worlds. Asians fantasise less overall, using play more to rehearse social conduct, such as how to be a good or bad child, parent or other family member*.

Fantasy play is more common in wealthier nations and in wealthier classes within nations. Where mothers in affluent nations work, they struggle to find time to play with their child, being more dominated by practicalities. Children in poor developing nations and children of working mothers in affluent ones spend more time watching television. However, research shows that even in societies where pretend play is actively discouraged, such as the Mayan communities of South America, children still attempt to engage in it: wherever it has been studied, some fantasy play is found on the part of small children.

Reviews of the educational advantages of play show that these are numerous*: It accelerates and enriches language development. Playful artistic creation can be helpful for small children who cannot yet form letters for writing, enabling them to get the habit of holding a brush (precursor to a pencil) and to concentrate on a task akin to writing on paper. If music is incorporated into the acquisition of mathematical concepts, it can accelerate higher performance in tests. But it is a common error to look upon the function of play as being primarily an educational one.

THE CONTENT OF PLAY REFLECTS PARENTING

What is ignored again and again in academic studies of play is that it expresses a small child's inner world. That world is, above all, dominated by the care the child is receiving from those upon whom it depends for its survival, both physically and mentally. The fact that play can have educational benefits is far less important than that it expresses the child's inner life, itself reflecting nurture.

Toddlers' strong drive to play can be dampened or extinguished by feelings of insecurity. This happens if there are no adults present who are loving and who meet physical needs in ways that match the child's unique wishes. John Bowlby's attachment theory predicts that under those circumstances, small children – those between the ages of 6 months and 3 years – become sad and angry, or just withdrawn*. They cease playing.

A significant proportion of parents are unable to be emotionally responsive for reasons such as depression, self-absorption (narcissism) or substance abuse. Some children, when small, are given inadequate substitute care for long periods of the day, because the parents are working. There is convincing evidence that this can cause distress*.

But if play can be discouraged or even extinguished by the care a small child receives, its greatest significance lies in what it expresses. Above all, the evidence shows that the content of children's play is profoundly affected by nurture.

Dozens of studies have shown that the content of children's narratives when creating imaginary stories reflects how they have been cared for*. In general, children who have been physically or sexually abused, or emotionally neglected, have more negative narratives than non-maltreated children. The maltreated portray bad things happening to them; they attribute bad intentions and anticipate negative responses more than the non-maltreated. That translates into destructive misperceptions of peers at school. Distressed and destructive themes in the play of 4- and 5-year-olds correlate with aggression and lack of impulse control when with other children*.

Narratives of maltreated children also demonstrate more dissociation than those of the non-maltreated*. Dissociation is feeling at one remove from oneself, distanced from feelings, as if one is merely an observer of one's life. It is also a confused state, in which one's own feelings and thoughts may be more easily mis-attributed to others. Dissociation has been shown to increase during the preschool period in maltreated children, but not in those who have not been maltreated. Normally, the self is increasingly integrated during the preschool period, but it becomes increasingly fragmented among the maltreated. The narratives of children with divorced parents reveal similar dissociation*.

What would the childhood narratives of Bowie and Terry have been about? It is highly probable that Bowie would have been aware of the tension between his parents; their coldness would have been registered, likewise the abuse he suffered at the hands of Kristina, his cousin. The maltreatment of Terry might have featured too, along with his sense of being entitled and special, about which there might have been guilt. There might also have been signs of dissociation.

As for Terry, his neglect on the part of Margaret and his growing sense of being unwanted would doubtless have featured strongly.

These narrative contents would have been the forebears of the thoughts and feelings both boys were to have as adults.

CHILDHOOD PLAY NARRATIVES CAN BECOME ADULT SYMPTOMS OF MENTAL ILLNESS

It is hard to exaggerate the importance of the evidence that the care children are given is reflected in their narratives, because they make sense of *adult*, as well as child, emotional distress. Specific kinds of childhood narrative content reflect specific kinds of maltreatment. These imaginary narratives, proven to express the kind of care children are receiving, may similarly explain the 'symptoms' of the 'mentally ill'. The repeated experience of childhood maltreatment results in these narrative contents converting into predictable symptoms when the child becomes a psychotic adult. Six studies

have shown that at least half the content of the hallucinations and delusions of adolescents or adults who had been
maltreated as children relate directly to its content*. Decades
later, when clients describe their adult distress, they are often
talking about maltreatment in the more or less distant past.

Adult 'symptoms' of 'mental illness' are, in fact, just like
the narratives of children. There are strong indications that
specific childhood maltreatment leads to specific adult difficulties*. One of the clearest pieces of evidence for this is the
connection between specific kinds of childhood maltreatment
and two symptoms of psychosis: paranoia and auditory hallucinations (hearing voices that are not really there).

Paranoid delusions are of imagined threats; they entail
a mistaken, pervasive assumption that others have malign
intentions towards one. The most common comment preced-
ing a city-centre violent crime is 'What are you looking at?'*.
In many cases, the person to whom the question is addressed
is not 'looking' at anything. But the paranoid person, imagining that the eyes or gestures of another person express a
criticism or some other hostile thought, may defend himself
by punching his imagined enemy's lights out. In children,
such paranoid attributions have been shown to be strongly
associated with physical abuse from parents or with other
coercive, negative care*. Early neglect is also associated with
paranoia: the person tends to assume the worst of others and
that they will deprive or frustrate him. People who are inse-
curely attached as a result of a lack of early care*, or who have
been victimised (either by being unfavoured in the family or
because of gender or race)*, or have been rendered powerless
by early care or subsequent experience*, are at greater risk of
paranoia.

In the case of hallucinations, severe early trauma in particular seems to interfere with the capacity to distinguish

between what is inner and what is outer: thoughts or feelings that are normally experienced as internal can be seen or heard outside oneself and may be attributed to more or less imaginary external entities, be they inanimate objects, such as paintings, or people.

A man I once interviewed was coming up the steps of Leicester Square underground station in London when he saw someone whose face he believed to be that of his father. His father had beaten him up frequently as a child, so, filled with rage towards his father, he attacked the man – a complete stranger. Similarly, Joseph Fischer, a serial killer I interviewed in America who claimed to have killed 161 people, felt that his mother had badly deceived his father, as well as having frequently beaten Joseph. She was a prostitute, and he hated the fact that she had gone with other men. When killing his victims, sometimes he would call them a whore, seeing his mother's face on theirs.

There is persuasive evidence that the more extreme and frequent the abuse, the greater the likelihood of a psychotic person having hallucinations. This is because the severely abused are more likely to experience dissociation* – which is a key factor in the development of psychosis. Faced with intolerably frightening and disturbing childhood abuse, they check out, observing themselves from a distance. Many survivors of sexual abuse report feeling that they left their bodies during the abuse and observed the events from the safety of the ceiling. In later life, their capacity to distinguish between what is inner and what is outer is looser: it is easier for them to conflate their internal thoughts and feelings about a situation with what is going on outside them.

Sexual abuse can be the most confusing, especially where penetrative sex has been experienced repeatedly, at a young age and on the part of a close relative. If a parent pushes a body part into the child, it may undermine the sense of what is 'me' and what is 'you'.

It is further confusing because it breaks social rules. A child is taught that it should not touch others' genitalia, let alone push parts of its body into other children. The incest taboo is more or less subtly communicated in all families, without being explicitly explained. If a child is coerced into sexual activity with a family member, it is crossing a fundamental social boundary that it knows to be forbidden. This is a chaotic boundarylessness, blurring identity.

MADNESS AS CONTAMINATION OF THE REAL WITH THE PRETEND

Maltreatment causes the breaking of the demarcation children need to have between reality and pretence in imaginative play. In order to safely allow a banana to be a telephone, the child must enter the pretend zone in which almost anything can be anything. So long as it does this, when back from the zone it will not pick up bananas when the actual phone rings. But suppose that quarantine is not firmly established in a child because it has been maltreated. It leads to a shaky grasp of what is real and what is illusion. In later life, when the person becomes distressed, he might be at greater risk of developing the delusions found in psychosis: the quarantine has collapsed, and it becomes more likely that he can hear voices.

Ordinary children's play does not entail hallucinations, only imaginary people and entities (monsters, fairies). If the quarantine is broken down in a child, it might start to live in a permanently magical world in which the imagined is as real as the real. This may be what happens in psychosis, and, if there has been sexual abuse, the specific symptom of hallucination may be more likely than other delusions, like seeing Jesus Christ or imagining you can hear the voices of conspirators out to get you.

There is good evidence that dissociation plays a particularly important role in promoting hallucinations in those who have been sexually abused*. Dissociation has been described as a loosening of the moorings in inner and outer reality. This is a collapse of quarantine between what goes into the pretend and real boxes, leading to inner imaginings and external reality becoming more easily mixed up. For the psychotic, it is as if dreams and waking life become indistinguishable, or as if a child's game of pirates is no longer understood as different in kind from ordinary life. In the absence of quarantine, the psychotic has made the leap back into the pretend zone without realising it is only the imagination at work. It is easy to see how confused, distressed people whose quarantine of the real from the pretend has broken down would actually hear their thoughts, or see them, experience them as really there, although outside rather than inside them.

As regards paranoia and hallucinations, a study based on a representative sample of over 7,000 Britons has strongly suggested that different kinds of childhood experience predict them*. It found that people who had suffered penetrative rape (rather than suggestive sexual talk or touching of genitals) before the age of 16 were fully six times more likely to have had auditory hallucinations (hearing voices that did not exist) in the last twelve months, than those who had not, but they were not more likely to have suffered paranoia.

The study also found that people brought up in institutional care were eleven times more likely to be paranoid. Being raised in an orphanage, where care is erratic and emotional needs are very rarely met adequately, almost always leads to great emotional insecurity – a foundation of paranoia.

People who had suffered physical abuse were at greater risk of both paranoia and hallucinations, though not to the same extent. This is not surprising: being hit about in childhood can well lead to a mind-set in which you expect aggression from others.

Sure enough, as found in nine other studies*, the more adverse childhood events a person had suffered, the greater the person's risk of suffering psychotic symptoms. As noted in Chapter 2, the risk of suffering psychosis is dose-dependent: the greater the dose of bad things happening in childhood, the greater the risk.

BOWIE'S CONVERSION OF HIS FEAR OF MADNESS INTO PLAY THROUGH PERSONAS

Bowie's childhood disturbed him considerably. The single greatest fear of which he was conscious was that of madness, having witnessed the madness of one of his aunts (Una) and, subsequently, Terry's disintegration. What he feared most was that his grandmother's curse upon the family was true: that he had inherited 'bad seed', and these genes would drive him mad.

When his grandmother and mother had had their blazing row, it was a struggle to apportion blame. Of course, scientifically speaking, blame is the wrong concept altogether. When Margaret withdrew into herself and was unable to meet the needs of her daughters as infants, or those of Terry, she did not intend to damage them. A series of studies has shown that parents whose children become schizophrenic had been twice as likely to put their own needs ahead of their child's as parents without a schizophrenic offspring (65%, vs 35%)*. Parents who are self-focused cannot be attuned to the needs of their infants, who suffer deprivation that is increasingly being regarded as a profound trauma that creates a basic fault line in identity development*. Often parents were unaware of putting their own needs first and had only been doing it as a way of coping, often in response to the way they themselves had been cared for as children.

Neither Margaret nor Peggy would have known anything about this research. With her 'bad seed' theory, Margaret was protecting herself from feeling guilty and from the accusations of her daughter. Peggy was expressing her fury at her mother for having neglected her. Such are the dynamics of families, and they pass down the generations*.

The legacy for Bowie was reported by Mary Finnigan, who was, in the late 1960s, a close intimate of his as well as his lover. Bowie told her that he had a fear of 'losing control'. Talking of madness, he said he was 'very marginal' (an astute assessment: personality disorder is on the borders of the sanity–madness line). More precisely, he told her that he believed that the fact that his eyes were mismatched was a sign of his potential insanity, and that he had 'had them from birth'. The mismatch had, in fact, been the consequence of a punch he had received from a friend in his mid-teens. Whatever the reason for this lie, it suggests that Bowie did believe that he had a genetically inherited tendency towards madness.

The period during which he was most at risk, between early 1974 and March 1976, was a result of consuming industrial quantities of cocaine. During the 1974 *Diamond Dogs* tour he became noticeably volatile. A musician from the tour recalled that 'One minute he would be a wonderful sweet friend, somebody who was easy to talk to and fool around with. The next minute he was somebody who would burn through you with their eyes. It was quite a sudden switch.' By the following spring his condition had deteriorated into the sporadically delusional.

Staying at a friend's house in Los Angeles, he became convinced that he was the victim of Black Magic. The home was near the house where the Manson Murders had occurred (in which the actress Sharon Tate was killed). When his friend dropped by, Bowie was convinced that the whole Manson 'family' were still at large (they had long been imprisoned, after the killings); there were knives hidden around the house with which he was intending to protect himself. Bowie also often spoke at that time of seeing ghosts. He told a journalist of frequent UFO sightings, and that these remained secret only because the population had been programmed by code words to disbelieve anything of which their controllers disapproved. On one occasion he phoned a friend whilst in a cocaine frenzy, convinced that there were groupies (he slept with many over the years) who were wanting him to impregnate them in order to create 'devil babies'.

At around that time, during the filming of the movie *The Man Who Fell To Earth*, he spent two days in hospital after seeing 'swirling liquid gold' in some milk. The film's director, Nicolas Roeg (with whom I hung out a bit in the 1980s), explained to me many years later that all he had to do was let Bowie be himself for him to play Thomas Jerome Newton, the lead role in the film. It is about an alien who has come to earth in a vain attempt to save his family but is widely misunderstood by humans. It ends with Bowie/Newton as a stupefied drunk, his head bowed on a café table. When the waiter comes to offer another drink, Newton's friend ironically tells the waiter, 'I think Mr Newton has had enough'. By that point, in his real life, Bowie was indeed as close to self-destruction as he would ever be.

Excessive cocaine use can result in psychotic episodes, though these seem to be different in form and content from ones not induced by drugs*. Bowie has described how extremely he abused the drug at that point. In the famous BBC documentary *Cracked Actor*, he is wafer-thin, audibly and visibly sniffing a lot in the characteristic way of people whose nasal passages are dried out and damaged by ingestion of the powder through the nose. In 1976, speaking of this period of cocaine addiction, he said: 'I started getting really, really worried for my life and I had to get myself out of that situation.' More recently, he commented that 'I just did too much [cocaine] and I came several times close to overdosing. It was like being in a car and the steering had gone, going over the edge of a cliff. I had almost resigned myself that I was not going to be able to stop.' He had adopted a persona that was in danger of causing his disintegrating; but, he said, in 1978, 'I took that image off. I put it in a wardrobe in an LA hotel and locked the door.'

Unlike Terry, Bowie had just enough of a sense of self to hang on during the dodgem-car ride that his turmoil became. Instead of resisting, he embraced it, using his considerable intellect and the façade of confidence his favoured status had conferred upon him. Although there were times when the pretend and the real came perilously close to merging, he never lost control for too long, or in the wrong times or places.

Terry had none of this mental kit. He probably had every bit as great an intellectual potential at conception and, given the right encouragement, could also have developed enough confidence to find vehicles for his demons. Instead of being nurtured, however, he had mainly been made to feel unwanted and rejected. The origin of his vulnerability lay in the unresponsive care he received from Margaret. But his capacity to use play to save himself was also insufficient. He could not use his imagination to invent the fictional worlds with which Bowie faced his horrors, and the illusion became delusion.

If most exceptional achievement in all fields derives from childhood adversity, so does nearly all mental illness. Terry passed through the door marked *Madness*. Bowie opened it, took a good look around and then passed through to the adjoining one, marked *Artistic Self-Expression*.

SIX

From Jones to Bowie
to Ziggy

The Rise And Fall Of Ziggy Stardust And The Spiders From Mars was recorded in the autumn of 1971, Bowie's third album in twelve months, during a period of intense productivity and remarkable diligence.

Ziggy Stardust is a space alien who becomes a rock star, only to be destroyed by stardom. Bowie had been a stage name that was a persona for a real person, David Jones. Gradually, Bowie became a significant part of who Jones was, professionally and personally. Ziggy was a persona of a persona.

At the simplest level, through creating Ziggy, Bowie fulfilled his ambition of rock stardom. The album and the live performances that accompanied it turned Bowie from a little-known figure into an international brand. But the Ziggy persona meant a great deal more to the real David Jones than that.

In his previous three albums, Bowie had repeatedly discussed the motives of leaders and followers, of idols and their fans, and the misunderstood prophet. For example, 'Cygnet Committee' (from the *Space Oddity* album) is the ruminations of a messiah figure expressing himself in semi-biblical terms.

He loved his followers 'madly', and his soul has been drained dry by them. He crushed his heart to ease their pain, but they had no consideration for his welfare. He had shown them the light and bankrupted himself in every way, and they had used him and become strong. In language that becomes frenziedly violent and distressed, Bowie laments the illusions of the leader and his followers, eventually resolving the angst with the simple proposition that he wants to live – in every sense.

The power of leadership and fame was an enduring conundrum for Bowie. During his cocaine era in the mid-1970s, he flirted with fantasies of dictatorship. He was fascinated by Hitler's life and by the iconography and staging of the Third Reich, drawing on the ideas of Josef Goebbels in creating the set for his 1976 *Thin White Duke* tour. Speaking in 1974, doubtless with an element of facetiousness, he said that Ziggy Stardust 'could have been Hitler in England – it wouldn't have been hard . . . I think I might have been a bloody good Hitler. I'd be an excellent dictator. Very eccentric and quite mad.' Speaking in 1976, he said, 'I'd adore to be Prime Minister. And yes, I believe very strongly in fascism . . . people have always responded with greater efficiency under regimental leadership.' In a highly publicised return to England, he stood in an open-roofed, huge black Mercedes Benz to greet a crowd of fans and was perceived by many there to have made a Nazi salute. He also said, 'Hitler was one of the first rock stars because he staged a country', which suggests his primary interest: the power and showmanship of Hitler as a hypnotist of the masses.

Bowie's preoccupation with the mechanics of fame and power, the mutually parasitical relationship between star and fan, politician and voter, could have arisen from his early conviction that stardom was to be his. He was sure that it would happen in 1963, ten years before it actually did. Shortly before Ziggy made his name, he told a journalist, 'I'm going to be huge, and it's quite frightening in a way.' He seemed as certain of this as that the sun would rise the next day. But, as he told his cousin Kristina, he was curious why it was he, not his half-brother, who had been chosen for greatness – not mental illness: when Terry hallucinated Jesus telling him that he had been chosen for a special job, in what sense was he any more deluded than Bowie before he became famous?

Until 1973, Bowie did not rise to fame. Prior to then, how could he be sure his conviction of achieving it was any saner than Terry's delusion? For every person convinced they will reach the top, there are thousands who have the same belief, but are wrong. This is not delusion: that line is crossed if they declare that they are already famous when they are not. But it is a thin line, and for the vulnerable, like Bowie as well as Terry, hallucinating oneself as chosen is always a risk.

As in his previous albums, *Ziggy Stardust* agonises restlessly about why fans need their stars. A few years before he died, Bowie said that Ziggy 'turned himself into an idol that people could worship. It hadn't happened before in rock, only in cinema.' Soon after his first live performances, Ziggy clones started to appear at the concerts, dressed in pastiches of the garish and curious costume that Bowie's wife Angie had encouraged him to adopt. Bowie had invented a fiction in which young people sought an identity – a person they wanted to be – in their search for something that felt real to them. It became a cult, complete with worshippers.

Bowie was training with mime artist and dancer Lindsay Kemp, as described below. So he was conscious of how to act, and he used this knowledge to make both Bowie and Ziggy seem like persuasive idols and leaders. Much of the background to his thinking came from Constantin Stanislavski, who maintained that successful performance entailed authenticity on stage, not acting.* By authenticity, Stanislavski meant the true emotional state of the actor: acting made these internal states external. According to Stanislavski, great actors seem to actually live the experiences of the characters they portray. Simulating being sad or amorous does not make actors believable: rather, they need to make use of their personal histories, their memories of specific occasions. Acting is not pretending to be someone else: it means being oneself, but in a different situation and context. Actors need to transplant that self into what he called a 'magic-if' scenario: reliving past experience, but in another context – that of the drama. While being aware that the events on stage are nothing other than fictional, they could act 'as if' they were real – like the pretend of the playing child.

The 'magic if' enables adaptations or substitutions between events that evoke powerful emotional memories. For example, in playing a character saddened by something that does not evoke sadness in the actor, a moment in the actor's own life that did evoke sadness can be substituted, 'as if' that were happening instead.

To maintain the illusion, actors must stay in the reality of the fiction throughout: thinking about something else, or becoming their true selves while listening to other actors speak, would make the emotion unbelievable. They have to act as if the drama were real life – not knowing what the other actor would say next.

All of a performance has to be congruent with the actor's real bodily state, which must be closely monitored. If something is not true to the actor, the body will unwittingly give the game away. Mere pretence will show up as discordance between the words being spoken and the actor's posture, gesture, facial expression, skin tone and other subtle physical clues. Only by closely monitoring their bodies can actors find the necessary synchrony and ensure that they are staying in the right zone. Sweaty palms, shortness of breath and other signs can tell actors that they are staying authentic. Such responses occur in real life at moments of threat, and they should be present at the moments when the character is feeling them.

One theory of leadership maintains that there is much to be learnt from Stanislavski, and Bowie seems to have intuited these possibilities in the way he created his leader personas, both as Bowie and as Ziggy, anchoring them in deep feelings dating back to childhood*. Leaders need a variety of enacted selves for different circumstances. For the roles to be acted effectively, leaders have to be closely attuned to their physical state, exactly as an actor must – aware of butterflies in their stomachs, the headiness of elation, the queasiness of uncertainty. When speaking to large audiences, it's not what you say, it's the way that you say it that matters – content is quickly forgotten. The body gives off powerful signals of authenticity, or of a lack thereof.

Those who have what is called 'embodied authentic leadership' score low on measures of chameleonism and impression management; they do not see themselves primarily through the eyes of others. They do, however, have to be consummate actors, in Stanislavski's sense – otherwise they would be naïve.

President Obama is a magisterial example of this capacity for authentic acting. When speaking, he comes across as natural, not actorly. His 'A More Perfect Union' speech achieved its impact through its closeness to issues he genuinely believes important in his life. There is no sense of him working to perform, 'acting into' his delivery of the speech. He manages to physically embody what he is saying.

Hence, as with Stanislavski's method for actors, leaders must use important moments from their lives to build authenticity in choosing content and how they deliver their speeches. These moments must be precise enough to remind them vividly of the physical sensations that went with the emotions of the original experience. When that happens, the audience is enthralled, knowing that the leader is truly experiencing what he is conveying.

The content of a leader's performance has to connect with the hopes and motives of the audience. In Bowie's case, this was not hard, speaking as he was to young people who were often also struggling with isolation, lack of identity and fears of running out of control.

Authentic leaders who offer visions that may be genuine to them but do not speak to the audience may feel true to themselves, but they will fail to connect. They have to provide their followers with a desired identity. During the first five years of the 1970s, Bowie had a phenomenal capacity to connect with his audiences' preoccupations and feelings, as his personal predicament mirrored theirs.

Leadership is not necessarily a comfortable position. Those who experiment with personas are, in the long run, more successful at not seeming fake, while incorporating new ways of being. Rehearsing these clumsy, often ineffective, sometimes inauthentic selves seems uneasy at first – but gradually they discover the possibilities and repertoires they are capable of, constantly refining and evolving their performances, just as actors do.

It might be said that the three albums that preceded *Ziggy Stardust* were Bowie's rehearsal for his life's main leadership role. In publicly discussing in those albums his worries about what leadership might bring, and in also trying out a variety of different leadership mantles, he prepared himself for his starring role.

There were several wheels within wheels in the Ziggy persona.

At the first level, there was simply a fiction about an alien who longs to be a star and, through his special powers and his beauty, becomes one. Subsequently, he crashes and burns.

At the second level, life imitated art. Like Ziggy, Bowie was deliberately creating a persona through whom he would become famous. This was calculated, intended. He did not claim that the moment of his global fame had arrived before the release of any of his previous albums. It is a documented fact that did he claim it before Ziggy.

At the end of 1971, during a dinner with Dai Davies, his publicist, Bowie said that he had been reading Kenneth Anger's book about the scams and politics of the film business, *Hollywood Babylon** and explained that he was going to be the spokesperson of a new generation and offer them a manifesto. Davies told him of a recently emerged school of rock journalists who would be receptive: they were thinkers and considered their own writings as artistic as those they were writing about. Davies recalled that 'He'd read about Elvis and he'd read about Hollywood in the thirties and forties. And he was building a brand – before that language had even been invented.' Bowie spoke of the plans for publicising Ziggy Stardust (such as announcing his own bisexuality) with the absolute certainty that when the album was released in a few months' time, he would become a star. Although the newly released *Hunky Dory* was selling a paltry 2,000 copies a week at that time, the hardened and sceptical Davies said,

'He convinced me he was going to be massive.' Perhaps most significant of all, Davies recalls that 'he told me he was going to *be* Ziggy' (my emphasis).

This was the third level: for much of the time David Jones, a real person, also experienced himself to be a persona, called Bowie. This persona was about to have periods close to the delusion that he actually was yet another persona, Ziggy; and an international fiction, 'the rise and fall of Ziggy Stardust', would become very real for millions of fans, at least during the time they listened to the songs or watched his performances. Their collective suspension of disbelief enabled Jones/Bowie to turn his conviction that he would be famous in the future into present reality. It changed him from being potentially delusional about his importance, as Terry had been, but the means of this transition was a flirtation with true delusion: that he *actually was* Ziggy.

Bowie subsequently said that in Ziggy, 'I'd found my character . . . Ziggy was this kind of mythological priest figure and I only say that in retrospect because I didn't know what he was then.' Indeed, at the time, there were periods when Ziggy was more than a myth: Bowie was engulfed by the persona. His cousin Kristina said that to begin with, on the tour, 'I would watch him when he got off stage and afterwards I could see that he dropped the character' – much like any other actor who has entered into a role and exits it on leaving the stage. But as the tour went on, it became less and less easy to tell Ziggy and Bowie apart, let alone to find David Jones. Increasingly, it was not only fans who were relating to Bowie as Ziggy: members of the tour entourage did so too. Kristina felt that people really did think they were 'dealing with Ziggy, not David'. When he asked her to join his touring entourage, she declined, feeling that he needed someone who could relate to him as David Jones. By then there was a poster campaign with the words 'David Bowie *is* Ziggy Stardust'. Mick Woodmansay, the drummer from The Spiders, recalled that 'You'd come off stage and he'd do interviews as Ziggy – you'd be sat in a taxi with this alien. You'd ask a question and he'd look right through you. He had turned into Ziggy Stardust.'

Years later, Bowie said of that time:

> 'I fell for Ziggy too. It was quite easy to become obsessed night and day with the character. I *became* Ziggy Stardust . . .
>
> Everybody was convincing me that I was a Messiah, . . .
>
> I got hopelessly lost in the fantasy . . .
>
> I can't deny that the experience affected me in a very exaggerated and marked manner. I think I put myself dangerously near the line.' [my emphasis]

The line that he had come close to crossing was between the pretend and the real. It is spelt out by the pun in the title of his next album, *Aladdin Sane* (A lad insane), written while touring America performing Ziggy. He described the characters on that album as 'crazy . . . Ziggy in America'; in writing it, he said, he had 'run into a very strange type of paranoid person'.

Inventing Ziggy turned what could have been a delusion of grandeur – that his fame was a destiny – into reality. It meant that he was not imagining things, whereas Terry had imagined that Jesus had chosen him. In the process, Bowie – itself a fictional name – came close to believing that he was indeed an imaginary rock 'n' roll star called Ziggy. Had he actually crossed that line, then the madness that engulfed Terry would also have been his: he would have been as delusional as his brother. However – as he had foreseen in the song 'The Man Who Sold The World' – he never lost control. This was expressed in the grand climax of the album, the song 'Rock 'N' Roll Suicide'.

The first song on the *Ziggy Stardust* album, 'Five Years', evokes a period before apocalyptic war and destruction. The rest of the first side sets the scene for the arrival of a messiah who can save the listener, a 'Starman' (whose chorus, incidentally, is a shameless lifting of the chorus from 'Somewhere Over The Rainbow', from *The Wizard of Oz*). On the second side, the future star emerges, musing how wonderful it will be to achieve stardom, with constant shifts in 'point of view' within the lyrics, from Bowie himself, to Ziggy, to Ziggy's fans. There are frequent references to the promiscuous sexual opportunities of the star and his grandiosity as he makes love 'with his ego'. His predatory use of women and overblown self-regard result in a leper messiah who is killed by the fans; the band is broken up. But then comes the climactic last song, 'Rock 'N' Roll Suicide'.

It begins with a simple acoustic-guitar melody, Ziggy wandering home in the early morning, lonesome and suicidal. But throughout the album, Bowie (and probably Jones as well) has appeared as a commentator on events. The music swells in a powerful crescendo then suddenly stops, and we hear Bowie's voice ring out, telling Ziggy that he is not alone. Bowie consoles Ziggy that he is watching himself but is too unfair, that his mind is all messed up and that the knives will lacerate his brain if he does not cease his self-loathing. Then Bowie calls out to him, telling him to hang onto him, to give him his hand – he, Bowie will protect Ziggy. The narrator moves from second person to first: 'I'll take my share, I'll help you with the pain.' Bowie ends by consoling Ziggy with the loving words, 'you're wonderful'. The whole is the performance of a divided self.

Of course, for many of the audience, the 'you' in the song represents them: they feel that Bowie is speaking about them and their loneliness. When the narrator shifts to the first person, it becomes even more personal: Bowie will take his share, he will help them with their pain. So when singing the song, Bowie is simultaneously resolving his personal anguish and making himself a star through a song that speaks to the thousands in the audience and the millions who eventually listened to the album.

The first live performance of Ziggy took place in England in February 1972; the album was released in June. In the autumn a tour of America began, with a mass of hype about this largely unknown performer (Bowie or Ziggy). Within three concerts, the kindling was laid, and by Christmas the fire had caught. In the New Year, Ziggy inflamed New York and Los Angeles. Easter 1973 found him performing in Japan to packed audiences already kitting themselves out in Ziggy costumes.

What was striking was that from early on in the live performances the song that the fans would respond most intensely to was 'Rock 'N' Roll Suicide'. Bowie developed the habit of moving down to the edge of the stage when he was telling Ziggy to take his hand, and the audience would literally reach out to him with theirs. Never a touchy-feely person and always holding something back, even from intimates, this was Bowie allowing himself to have contact with others, in both senses, emotionally as well as physically. He had sung in earlier songs of the need to turn and face the stranger: now he was doing it very publicly. At times, perhaps, the 'he' who was doing that may have been David Jones.

The song was about a very real issue for its author. Bowie was all too aware that suicide presented a significant risk for rock stars, although at the time when he began portraying Ziggy Stardust hard drugs had not played a major part in his life. The year 1970 had seen the deaths of Jimi Hendrix, Janis Joplin and Jim Morrison. Bowie had smoked his fair share of marijuana and dabbled a little with heroin, but he never dangerously indulged in either. He had been at pains to avoid the hallucinogen LSD. As a song, 'Rock 'N' Roll Suicide' was a clever warning to himself, or a part of himself. Jim Morrison had sung of The End being his only friend. Bowie reached out to save Ziggy and reconnect with Jones. He had already predicted that he would never lose control completely, and there is an interesting study of rock suicides giving grounds for that confidence*. It suggests that it is not fame that makes stars so prone to emotional problems – mostly it is childhood maltreatment and adversity. Other studies had already proven that, compared with the general population, rock and pop stars tend to die prematurely. There is persuasive evidence that the creative are more psychotic*. This study examined a sample of 1,210 stars voted as the creators of the most popular albums in America or Europe since the 1950s, who had achieved a minimum of five years of fame. Of these, 9% died prematurely.

Solo performers were twice as likely to die prematurely as those in bands. Bowie grew increasingly remote from his musicians as he withdrew behind the Ziggy mask, and this made him especially vulnerable. But the crucial finding was that the reason for the deaths could be traced to adverse childhood experiences* (ACEs: experiences like parental divorce or maltreatments like emotional neglect or abuse).

A key factor is that ACEs increase the likelihood of substance abuse. Twice as many of the stars who died from substance abuse had at least one ACE, compared with those who died of other causes. Of those who died from substance abuse, 80% had two or more ACEs.

This is exactly what studies of the general population would predict. Having four or more ACEs makes you seven times more liable to abuse alcohol and twelve times more likely to attempt suicide. The number of ACEs has also been shown to be a major cause of personality disorders like narcissism, which have, in turn, been proven to be more common on the part of both fame-seekers* and the famous*.

The number of ACEs probably also explains why stars who do survive into middle age tend to die prematurely. Childhood adversity is a major cause of other diseases: people with four or more ACEs are twice as likely to suffer from cancer and heart disease. One reason is that high-ACE people abuse substances more, which, in turn, greatly increases the incidence of those diseases. Indeed, Bowie was to suffer a heart attack in 2004, possibly because cocaine abuse had damaged his cardio-vascular system. But he did not die – perhaps because he had stepped back from the cocaine precipice, and so the damage was insufficient to kill him: although it was a close-run thing, he never lost control. It is nonetheless possible that his recent death from cancer had been hastened by his substance abuse.

In the conclusion of their paper on ACEs, the authors point out that 'pursuing a career as a rock or pop musician may itself be a risky strategy and one attractive to those escaping from abusive, dysfunctional or deprived childhoods'. In Bowie's case, his childhood had been dysfunctional enough for him to be at risk, but not so bad that he would kill himself.

A further body of evidence illustrates the danger in which Bowie placed himself through his stardom and the insightfulness he was showing in 'Rock 'N' Roll Suicide'*. A study of the entire Swedish population looking back over the last 30 years shows that suicide is three times more common among children whose parents had died that way. This is not the result of genes: children who lose parents through physical illness are not at greater risk – it is the manner of the death that plants the idea of repeating it. While rates of being hospitalised with depression are considerably increased in children who have lost parents in accidents or through illness, actual suicide is not more likely.

Further evidence that suicide is contagious comes from suicidal clusters identified in groups of doctors, police and farmers. Since 2007, the rate of suicide has risen steadily in the American military. In 2012, more died by their own hand (349) than in combat. By no means was this all due to the trauma of war. Half of the military suicide personnel had never been deployed. Contagion seems to be the cause of the rise.

Contagion is also rife in schools and universities: the suicide of one student increases the risk of further suicides in that institution. When celebrities or characters in television fictions kill themselves, the vulnerable are put at risk: people of the same gender and age as the celebrities or TV characters commit suicide in greater numbers in the succeeding months.

Given the proximity of the deaths of the likes of Jim Morrison to the point at which Bowie both predicted and achieved fame, he was quite right to fear suicide as an outcome. Contagion does not happen only between celebrities and their fans; it may well be between celebrities themselves.

As well as fear of death by his own hand, from before he became famous Bowie was haunted by the idea that he was going to be assassinated by a fan on stage. He sensed the danger of leadership, the way in which it could make him a target of envy. During one of the performances of Ziggy, a fan ran onto the stage, and Bowie collapsed in a faint, terrified that he was about to be killed.

After the murder of John Lennon in 1980, Keith Richards carried a gun. Bowie got Gary, a muscular ex-US Navy Seal. He also attended a media course for dealing with the public and was an eager student. It taught him how to deal with

casual encounters on the street and mapped out danger signals in letters and other communications. When he suffered
his heart attack in 2004, he was on-stage – a variant of his
worst nightmare nearly coming true. But in the case of Ziggy,
it was to be Bowie who killed him.

The first performance of Ziggy Stardust had been in 1972.
Only 18 months later, on 3 July 1973, at the Hammersmith
Odeon in London, Bowie spoke to the audience just before
singing 'Rock 'N' Roll Suicide'. Normally, there was no break
between the sexed-up 'wham, bam, thank you ma'm' frenzy of
the previous song, 'Suffragette City', and the sharply contrast-
ing simplicity of the few acoustic guitar chords with which
'Suicide' opens. Now Bowie broke off to make an announce-
ment: 'Not only is it the last show in the tour, but it's the
last show we'll ever do.' He then sang the song and, to the
amazement of his musicians, who had had no warning of
this development, disbanded his backing group, The Spiders
From Mars. Even more pertinently, he removed the mask and
apparel of Ziggy.

He was, however, not finished with the adoption of personas: he created new ones for three of his next four albums
(*Aladdin Sane, Diamond Dogs* and *Station To Station*). But he
had expressed what he needed through Ziggy and was sane
enough to realise that the persona had served its purpose.
In 1978, referring back to his decision to give up drugs, live
performances and persona-based albums, he said, 'It just
needed a positive decision to only do things that I wanted to
do and not for the sake of "David Bowie" or "The Thin White
Duke" or whoever I was playing at the time was expected to
do.' Ziggy had enabled Bowie to reconnect with Jones. He
explained that 'It helps to recognise the angels and devils in
yourself, I think . . . my moods change such a lot, so drasti-
cally, and even my persona privately changes a lot . . . as long

as you keep recognising it, stand outside whoever's taken over at the time and the other one stands outside and has a look.' Many therapists would agree heartily with these thoughts.

Through adopting personas, Bowie succeeded in changing who he was. He did this through integrating his childhood experiences into the adults he pretended to be. Many of Bowie's public utterances are playfully flippant or whimsical or teasing. But I suspect that the following statement of his was heartfelt and was intended to be taken seriously:

'You have to accommodate your pasts within your persona . . . it helps you reflect what you are now.'

While the lyrics of Ziggy do not delve into Bowie's family history directly, they are his attempt to deal with the legacy of madness it passed on to him.

Peggy, Bowie's mother, was an attractive woman who placed high value on the power of her appearance to interest men. As a mother, her only material contribution to Terry's upkeep while he was being raised by her was to purchase expensive and tasteful clothing for him. She similarly insisted from the start that Bowie was neatly, smartly dressed. He showed a strong interest from a young age in both his clothing and his coiffure, as did Terry, his model.

As a teenager, Bowie was conscious of his desirability and the power it gave him over girls. As soon as he began playing in bands, he embarked upon a career as a highly promiscuous lothario, which continued until his forties (discussed in Chapter 8). Pretences and appearances fascinated him. The boy who had been characterised as 'an exhibitionist' in his final school report had been his parents' favourite. In key respects, for them he could do no wrong, and his sense of his own value was inflated. However cold his mother had been when he was small and however uncomfortable they both were with physical expressions of affection, he had always been cast by them as the clever, adorable, sweet little boy. He also had going for him that he was exceptionally good-looking, in every way.

But it was not until he met Lindsay Kemp, the mime artist and dancer, that he understood the artistic potential of personas. Kemp had trained with Marcel Marceau in Paris and had set up a dance company in London. After seeing Kemp perform in 1967, Bowie telephoned him, asking for a meeting. A homosexual, Kemp was astonished by Bowie's beauty, calling him 'an angel'. As Bowie's tutor and lover, Kemp helped him to lose his inhibitions as a performer and to realise the potential of theatricality and display. When Kemp created a show based around him, Bowie grasped the power of dance and of eccentric clothing as ways to manipulate audiences.

His professional relationship with Kemp prepared him for another key experience in the development of his interest in personas: exposure to the New York of Andy Warhol and Lou Reed. Bowie had become absorbed in the hazy thinking, droopy clothing and uncouth hair of the mid-1960s (celebrated by 'Memory Of A Free Festival' on *Space Oddity*), living in communes, smoking marijuana and dressing as a hippy. But by August 1971, when he first encountered Warholism at first hand, he had already started wearing dresses and adopted some of the other camp habits that were to make him the icon of glam rock. *Pork*, a controversial play performed by Warhol acolytes, was showing in London, and one of the actors contacted Bowie, who was enthralled by anyone with proximity to Warhol.

The play portrayed outrageous sexuality, and Bowie was fascinated by its multiple levels. The actors were not formally trained, and many of them were rebelling against highly conventional middle-American backgrounds. They had joined radical theatre groups in New York and been encouraged to use their real personalities to create their roles. Tony Zee, the man who was performing the role of Warhol in *Pork*, described the blurring of the real and the imaginary it entailed: 'I began to get into my own fantasy of me as Warhol and people related to me as if I was. We were beginning to play these people, beginning to act like they did, although we were still playing ourselves.' Zee noticed that this idea of enacting oneself captured Bowie's interest: 'It was a lot about role-playing, and David was lured in the same way, because he was in the process of doing the same thing.'

A month later, Bowie went to New York and visited Warhol's famous studio, The Factory. The lack of any chemistry between the two is all too visible in a film taken of the visit*. When Bowie played Warhol a recording of his *Hunky Dory* song 'Andy Warhol', there was a sense of humour-failure. Although a tribute to the artist, the song is teasingly playful in a way that Warhol seems to have been unable to cope with ('That was great – thank you very much', he stiffly responded). Bowie had more joy with Lou Reed, for whom he was to create Reed's best-selling and sexually ambiguous persona – the one on the cover of the album *Transformer*, which Bowie somehow found the time to successfully produce for his friend in 1972.

The experiences with Lindsay Kemp and with the Warhol acolytes were crucial in opening Bowie's eyes to the artistic potential of pretence – especially personas that were both he and not he. The idea of performing roles that could transform (transformers) was central to his work from Ziggy onwards.

In 2015, Bowie described himself as 'a collector, a collector of personalities'. He turned the creation and adoption of personas into a form of therapy. Clinically, this is done through drama or art therapy, through which clients discover and explore distressing experiences, assisted by a therapist. Bowie did it for himself through his musical career.

Crucially, he said that:

> 'I decided to enact a lot of the material I had written rather than perform it as myself.'

Many other stars did not pretend to be someone else when performing, nor did they invent characters in their lyrics. Lennon's 'Strawberry Fields' or McCartney's 'Penny Lane' were personal testaments by people who went by the same name as the ones on their birth certificates. While The Beatles did create several albums with fictional narrative components (*Sergeant Peppers' Lonely Hearts Club Band*, *Yellow Submarine*, *The Magical Mystery Tour*), they never intended them as therapy. (In fact, the fictions were mostly – relatively unsuccessful – expressions of McCartney's sentimental love of nostalgia.)

Popular musicians have long been prone to adopting stage names, and many rock musicians have since adopted personas (from Elvis Presley to Madonna to Lady Ga-Ga), some hoping to imitate Bowie's commercial success as a showman. But in most cases artistically they fell far short of Bowie's music and his performances, starting with Ziggy in 1972 to his last persona-based tour in 1976 as The Thin White Duke.

The difference was that Bowie was using personas to understand his current psychology and its history. Like most art of any profundity, it was an expression of his inner conflicts – but in his case it was a desperate and more or less deliberate attempt to use personas to overcome them. Ziggy may have started life as a gag through which to achieve fame, but he was also the culmination of Jones's struggle to experience madness in a safe way, much as the schizophrenese of his lyrical style was a way for him to be safely psychotic. It was a means to develop multiple personalities without becoming a case of multiple personality disorder. It converted the potential delusion that he was to become famous into a reality. It grappled with the predicament created by the idolatry he would encounter as a famous leader. But, above all, as with the previous albums, it was anchored in his family history. The persona therapy that was the Ziggy project was his way of dealing with his family's myth of genetically transmitted intergenerational madness and of addressing his personality disorder, caused by the way his parents had cared for him.

As we shall see in the next chapter, multiple personalities are available to all of us, not just to artists like Bowie or to people who are diagnosed as suffering from multiple personality disorder.

SEVEN

From multiple normal personas to multiple personality disorder

In playing with personas, Jones was living dangerously, but in his case it might have been even more of a risk *not* to do so: he needed to find a way to express and understand the legacy of his family politics and childhood adversities. It is important to understand that, through Bowie and Ziggy, Jones was only doing what all of us do, to a greater or lesser extent: he was just achieving it more extremely and with greater dexterity. In this chapter, I show that Jones's life of multiple personas was not as different from normal as it might seem. Realising this has big implications for how we should regard ourselves.

THE DEVELOPMENT OF PERSONAS

In developed nations we take it for granted that we have many different personas – at home, at work, and so on – yet in the longer sweep of history such multiplicity is a recent development. In the simplest societies, groups of 30 to 40 people hunt and gather their daily food; they do not live in any settled, single location. Such societies are almost extinct today, but for most of human history they were the only social structure. There was no settled agriculture, and there were so few people that it was possible to eat the produce of local plants and trees, kill local animals, and then simply up sticks and move to another location*.

In such small communities, there was far less need for multiple personas. Everyone was related by blood to everyone else, everyone knew everyone's name, and they knew virtually everything about each other. Beliefs about nature, society and how to conduct oneself were uniform and shared. Putting on masks was unnecessary.

We now live in a much more complex system, one that requires us to develop different faces for different settings, starting with school, on to university and into the workforce. We often move away from the place of our birth, and we meet hundreds of new people from diverse backgrounds. With the advent of the Internet, the potential for meeting and keeping in touch with people from all over the world has expanded exponentially.

In primary school, the child's social circle remains relatively small, restricted to family, friends of family and other pupils. However, in the teenage years, at secondary school, the number of acquaintances expands greatly. The development of flexibility of traits depending upon situation accelerates. As William James, the famous nineteenth-century psychologist, put it: 'A man has as many social selves as there are individuals who recognise and carry an image of him in their mind. . . . Many a youth who is demure enough before his parents and teachers, swears and swaggers like a pirate among his "tough" young friends'*. This is borne out in key studies by Susan Harter and colleagues*. She prefaces her findings by pointing out that our multiple selves can live in harmony: 'An army officer might be stern with his soldiers, yet tender with his children.

The refined poet may fashion exquisite verses during the day but be a foul-mouthed, coarse drunk that same evening.'

Problems can arise if the various selves are too discordant and contradictory. Many adolescents feel themselves pulled in different directions by differing opinions and emotions. While we can be consistent in our relationships with the same friends or relatives, part of development is grasping that we cannot afford to be the same in all situations and with everyone we meet: we have to develop different identities to cope with the roles of student, offspring, employee, romantic companion.

The difficulty is that, if our autonomy is not being expressed as we hop between personas, a lack of meaning will increasingly make itself felt. This meaninglessness is a recurring theme in nineteenth- and twentieth-century literature, in the work of Dostoyevsky, Tolstoy and Chekhov, as well as the crescendo of nihilism, starting with Nietzsche, through Sartre, into the diverse depictions of alienation in the second half of the twentieth century, such as in J.D. Salinger's *The Catcher in the Rye*.

In her series of studies, Harter demonstrated that adolescents have different selves for each of their parents, for their siblings, for their close friends and their romantic partners. They will also show differing traits as students and in their jobs. They may be depressed and sarcastic with parents but caring and rowdy with friends. Curious and attentive as students, they may be self-conscious with romantic partners.

Age increases the rate of this proliferation of personas. Asked to define their attributes in different relationships and roles, adolescents may describe about 25–30% of traits in all roles in early adolescence, but only 10% later on. The sense of self-contradiction peaks in middle adolescence and drops slightly as the end of the teens approaches. They start to get used to the idea that they must be different.

Overall, the greatest sense of contradiction is in traits displayed to each parent, and in the difference in the ways they are with their parents as against with their friends. They are generally closer to their mother than to their father – more open with her, more secretive with him. Then they are puzzled at how short-tempered they might be with their mother, yet be such a good listener with romantic partners. They are quietly respectful if listening to father, yet assertive to friends.

TRUE AND FALSE SELVES

The more adolescents feel self-contradictory in their various roles, the greater their sense of difficulty in not being false – in expressing what they call their true self. This is described as 'the real me inside' and 'saying what you really think'. The false self entails 'being phoney' and 'not expressing my true opinions'.

The highest level of false selfhood is felt by daughters with their fathers – 40% of girls feel they are primarily false in that relationship*. The same proportion of girls attending all-girl schools will feel false when with boys. Then come false exchanges with classmates, teachers and friends (about one quarter feel false with these groups).

On two thirds of occasions where they feel false, this arises from a sense of self-contradiction. They might wish they were happy (seen as their true self) but be having to pretend (false self), because they are depressed. If they are normally patient (true self), impatience towards their mother will seem out of place (false self). Generally extrovert (true self), they find it perplexing how nervous and silent they become if out on a date (false self).

Harter shows that while it would actually be ridiculous to be equally self-revelatory to teachers or casual acquaintances as to friends, some find it harder than others to accommodate to this. The strongest predictor of who suffers is the extent to which false selves are dominant. Low self-esteem and depression are more likely in those who feel more false.

Harter offers several reasons why some feel false much of the time. One is a parental pattern of subtly tampering with the child's memory of what has happened to them, encouraging them to forget the way in which they have been treated. The incidents may be relatively minor, such as a parent having put the child under heavy pressure to succeed academically, or it might be much more extreme, such as physical or sexual abuse. The memory of this having been altered or suppressed by parents, a false version has been substituted, which the child believes to be real.

Another cause for a feeling of falseness may arise from parents making their love conditional on performance. This can start very early in life. If parents do not respond to infantile needs, then the baby may learn to fit itself to its carer, eventually suppressing cries of distress indicating its needs, such as for food or comfort. The infant who has given up crying may be described by its parent as a 'good baby' – in fact, it has developed a false self based on despair at ever having its needs met.

Authentically felt smiles (known as *Duchenne* smiles) use a range of facial muscles. These are not used in simulated smiling that signals pleasure or friendliness but is not felt. Babies, like adults, know intuitively from facial patterns when others are simulating. If their carer is not really feeling love when smiling at them, this trains them to fake their own smiles.

Only by pretending to be pleased by their carer may they get attention and at least a simulation of the love they need.

As children get older, parents may more or less subtly demand that they adopt their goals by showing genuine affection only if the child succeeds in achieving these. The prodigy in sport or music or academia has often been forced from a very young age to achieve to a high standard in order to be rewarded with love. The achievements can then feel very false to them. More broadly, lack of emotional attunement on the part of parents can lead to false ways to get the parent's attention.

If a parent coerces the child by slapping, hitting or through other violence, or the threat thereof, this can cause the true self to go underground. The child is forced to fit in with the parent, to simulate what it believes the parent requires.

All these patterns, alone or in combination, tend to result in the person not knowing what is real and what is true for them. For example, if a child has been persistently hijacked by its parents' ambitions and has become a high achiever, then it may have no idea that its desire to be a great golfer or a top politician has little to do with its own authentic impulses. Such people may enthusiastically claim that they love their profession and have no idea that they are in fact a hologram of their parents' ambitions.

Children whose parents have been consistently very negative, hitting them and telling them that they are failing (even though they may have come second in the highest class at school), may come to believe that their true self is a helpless, hopeless, inadequate person and that their achievements or merits are false.

Where parental care has to be concealed from outsiders because it has involved sexual or physical abuse that will get the parent into trouble, secret pacts are forced upon the child.

It may be persuaded that it has been abused for its own good and that the abuse is deserved. In such cases, the child may feel its true self is rotten to the core and must therefore be concealed from others at all costs. An abused child sees its negative attributes as authentic and central components of what it is like, whereas children from less toxic homes see their positive attributes as these components*.

The more extreme the maltreatment endured, the greater the likelihood of developing a severely fragmented personality, as the different selves are kept in separate boxes. Not only must the disgusting, loathsome self that forced the parent to maltreat them be kept secret from outsiders, it must be concealed even from themselves. They can only afford to know about this degraded self in certain settings, such as with the abuser or, in later life, with a lover with whom they may partially relive the experience. The seeds have been sown for multiple personality disorder.

MULTIPLE PERSONALITY DISORDER

Multiple personality disorder (MPD, now known as dissociative identity disorder because the personalities are disconnected from each other) is identified as a distinct form of mental illness. As we shall see, it is far from being the extreme abnormality it is presented as in the textbooks. There is a spectrum, with illusions at one end and delusions at the other.

At the healthiest extreme are children's pretences during solitary fantasy play in which they enact different characters. My son, even at the age of 9, liked to spend some time most evenings with a number of small toy men. He preferred privacy, since he felt a little old to be seen playing this game, but he spoke the actions of the characters – 'he crashes into

Paul, whammmm' – as he had them engaged in their warring. Younger children's play is unselfconscious – dolls being sat at tables, bears being placed in tents and all the other glories of pretend play*. Here we see a series of different characters in the child's mind enacting imaginary scenarios.

Next along the spectrum are the pretences of adults during conversation: putting on a funny voice, imitating accents in telling a story, making up imaginary events to fool a friend as part of a joke – for brief moments, they may 'become' someone else.

Then there are all kinds of art and, most conspicuously, actors in dramatic productions. Sane adults inhabit characters of imaginary people, more or less feeling themselves to be those fictions. The audience are no less engaged, having suspended their disbelief, even crying tears or expressing rage in response to nonexistent persons.

Next comes the surprisingly common phenomenon of feeling like an impostor. This is the sense that you are liable to be tapped on the shoulder and exposed as someone who is impersonating yourself, or that although in reality you may know you have, say, qualified as a doctor, you often have the feeling that you are blagging and have not qualified at all. (Dreams of having failed exams that we have actually already passed are a common, normal form of this.)

Entering the realm of the psychiatric, we come to the as-if personality often found in borderline personality disorder. Here, people feel at their most real when they are only pretending to be themselves. For example, the disc jockey Tony Blackburn once told me that he felt most real for the period of time when he was the version of himself that performed on radio. He only wished that he could have that sense of heightened reality in the rest of his life, which felt relatively second-hand and empty. 'I wish my whole life could be a radio show', he told me.

At the end of the spectrum come fully fledged delusions, such as are found in psychoses. People who have these may believe that they are an entity different from the one named on their birth certificate, or they may meet hallucinated others, such as when Terry saw Jesus Christ. They may connect events that are unconnected, believing themselves to be victims of imaginary conspiracies. At times, they may not know who they are, living in a state of profound confusion.

But one stage back from full psychosis are cases of multiple personality disorders (well described by Nicholas Humphrey and Daniel Dennett, upon whom I draw extensively in what follows*). Typically, there is a host personality, the ringmaster for a number of others (alters). Generally, these personalities have different names. They may speak in various dialects, believe they live in different places, wear differing clothing. When David Jones 'became' Bowie, this may have had elements of an alter ego; when Bowie 'became' Ziggy, there were certainly moments or periods of time when this was a fully fledged alter, or, host.

Humphrey and Dennett state that,

> None of the personalities is emotionally well-rounded. The Host is often emotionally flat, and different Alters express exaggerated moods: Anger, Nurturance, Childishness, Sexiness. Because of their different emotional skills, it falls to different Alters to handle different social situations. Thus one may come out for lovemaking, another for playing with the kids, another for picking a fight, and so on.
>
> The Host is on stage most of the time, but the Alters cut in and displace the Host when for one reason or another the Host cannot cope. The Host is usually amnesic for those episodes

when an Alter is in charge; hence the Host is likely to have blank spots or missing time. Although general knowledge is shared between them, particular memories are not.

The life experience of each Alter is formed primarily by the episodes when she or he is in control. Over time, and many episodes, this experience is aggregated into a discordant view of who he or she is and hence a separate sense of self.

Humphrey and Dennett provide the example of "Mary", not based on a single person but a composite of various real ones. Hospitalised, she is in her early thirties and has been suffering from depression, confusional states and lapses of memory. Her therapist, a Doctor R, specialises in treating dissociative disorder, and a picture gradually emerges:

> Mary's father died when she was two years old, and her mother almost immediately remarried. Her stepfather was kind to her, although 'he sometimes went too far.' Through childhood she suffered from headaches. Her teenage years were stormy, with dramatic swings in mood. She vaguely recalls being suspended from her high school for a misdemeanor, but her memory for her school years is patchy. In describing them she occasionally resorts – without warning – to the third person ('She did this . . . That happened to her'), or sometimes the first-person plural ('We [meaning Mary] went to Grandma's'). She is artistically creative and can play the guitar, but when asked where she learned it, she says she does not know and deflects attention to something else. She agrees that she is 'absent-minded' – 'but aren't we all?' She might find there are clothes in her closet that she cannot remember buying, or discover she has sent her niece two birthday cards. She claims to have strong moral values; but other people, she admits, call her a hypocrite and liar. She keeps a diary 'to keep up with where we're at.'

Dr R noticed that Mary's diary's handwriting varied between entries. Usually demure, under hypnotism a different Mary emerges, saying 'Hi Doctor, I'm Sally . . . Mary's a wimp.'

As the sessions progress, Sally slips in and out of her sub-personalities, alluding to a promiscuous past. But when Mary reappears, she apparently has no knowledge of Sally. Subsequently, several other alters emerge – the angry Hatey and the child-like, easily influenced Peggy. Each of the alters has its own special memories and account of its life, as well as knowing about Mary's, but Mary does not know about them or their memories. To begin with, the transition between alters is signalled by a blankness in the eyes or placing her hands to cover them. Slowly it becomes possible for Dr R to ask Mary if a certain one is present and for it to emerge on request. From speaking with them, a coherent narrative of Mary's childhood adversities is pieced together:

> When Mary was four years old, her stepfather started to take her into his bed. He gave her the pet name Sandra, and told her that 'Daddy-love' was to be Sandra's and his little secret. He caressed her and asked for her caresses. He ejaculated against her tummy. He did it in her bottom and her mouth. Sometimes Mary tried to please him, sometimes she lay still like a doll. Sometimes she was sick and cried that she could take no more. One time she said that she would tell – but the stepfather hit her and said that both of them would go to prison. Eventually, when the pain, dirt, and disgrace became too much to bear, Mary simply 'left it all behind': while the man abused her, she dissociated and took off to another world. She left – and left Sandra in her place.

This Mary was able, to some extent, to function normally as she grew up, wholly unaware of what was being done to Sandra. Humphrey and Dennett continue,

> Mary's gain was however Sandra's loss. For Sandra knew. And this knowledge, in the early years, was crippling. Try as she might, there was no single story that she could tell that would embrace her contradictory experiences; no one 'Sandra-person'

for her to become. So Sandra, in a state of inchoateness, retreated to the shadows, while Mary – except for 'Daddy-love' – stayed out front.

Yet if Mary could split, then so could Sandra. And this, it seems, is what occurred. Unable to make it all make sense, Sandra made sense from the pieces – not consciously and deliberately, of course, but with the cunning of unconscious design: She parcelled out the different aspects of her abuse-experience, and assigned each aspect to a different self (grafting, as it were, each set of memories as a side-branch to the existing stock she shared with Mary). Thus her experience of liking to please Daddy gave rise to what became the Sally-self. Her experience of the pain and anger gave rise to Hatey. And her experience of playing at being a doll gave rise to Peggy.

Now these descendants of the original Sandra could, with relative safety, come out into the open. And before long, opportunities arose for them to try their newfound strength in settings other than that of the original abuse. When Mary lost her temper with her mother, Hatey could chip in to do the screaming. When Mary was kissed by a boy in the playground, Sally could kiss him back. Everyone could do what they were 'good at' – and Mary's own life was made that much simpler. This pattern of what might be termed 'the division of emotional labor' or 'self-replacement therapy' proved not only to be viable, but to be rewarding all around.

Subsequently this became the habitual way of life. Over time each member of the family progressively built up her own separate store of memories, competencies, idiosyncrasies and social styles. But they were living in a branching house of cards. During her teenage years, Mary's varying moods and waywardness could be passed off as 'adolescent rebelliousness.' But in her late twenties, her true fragility began to show—and she lapsed into confusion and depression.

In discussing the implications of this story for normality, Humphrey and Dennett propose an analogy between the different selves we have and a government. One of the selves is elected Head of State, but the others are important. Normally, as we grow up, having started with no particular sovereign, we gradually elect one to represent the many different aspects of ourselves – what we might think of as the true me. But in someone who has suffered severe childhood adversity, where there is too much competition between the different parts of the selves, there may be chaos, because they are unwilling to accept the outcome of elections, resulting in frequent *coup d'états*. As each insurrection occurs (for example, in the case of Mary), different parts of the prior experience demand to be expressed; and since Mary must not know about them, they take over, until satisfied. Mary was too chaotic and disorganised to remain as the leader: the Sandras, Peggys and other factions were able to overthrow her from time to time. Constitutionally unstable, it was hard for the person called Mary to know who she really was.

Humphrey and Dennett offer some striking examples of other people with MPD who show no awareness of their alters:

> One woman told us of when – as frequently happened – she came home and found her neat living room all messed up, she suspected that other people must be playing tricks on her. A young man described how he found himself being laughed at by his friends for having been seen around gay bars: he tried over several months to grow a beard to prove his manhood, but as soon as the stubble began to sprout, someone – he did not know who – shaved it off. A woman discovered that money was being mysteriously drawn from her bank account, and told the police that she was being impersonated. We have heard of a case of a highly skeptical patient who refused to accept her therapist's diagnosis until they both learned that one of her alters was seeing *another* therapist.

It is now widely accepted that MPD is a real phenomenon*. A particularly telling study was of a single case: a woman who underwent psychotherapy for 15 years*. Blind at the outset, she gradually regained her sight. However, only some of her personalities were sighted. When her brainwaves were measured, it was shown that when a sighted alter was hosting, the patterns of brainwaves in her visual cortex were normal, but they were not when it was a blind alter. This seems very powerful evidence that separate personas really do exist. It is also largely uncontested that MPD is caused by extreme childhood maltreatment. However, it would be a mistake to regard people who function like this as in a wholly different category from everyone else. Humphrey and Dennett go so far as to say that all of us have multiple personalities competing within us: the difference is that we are more aware of their existence, and one is accepted as the 'ruler', the arbiter of which of us will be on show at any one time. The difference for someone with MPD is that there is a continual battle going on for who is the spokesperson, with abrupt shifts that are not found in most of us. But there are important senses in which people with MPD illustrate what is 'normal'.

This is exemplified by the case of Kenneth Bianchi, who, along with his cousin Angelo Buono Jr, carried out eleven rape-murders in Los Angeles between October 1977 and February 1978 (they became known as the Hillside Stranglers). After his capture, despite being confronted with almost conclusive evidence of his guilt, he maintained his innocence. Bianchi had been adopted at the age of 3 months and had a deeply troubled childhood, which could have put him at risk of MPD.

Kenneth Bianchi was a handsome, charming and apparently friendly man. While being investigated by psychiatrists, he underwent hypnosis, which is the commonest means by which MPD emerges in therapy. During the course of this, a new Bianchi emerged, called Steve*. Steve – a savage, foul-mouthed, aggressive person – was a very different animal from Kenneth. For some time, it was believed that Bianchi was a case of MPD, similar to the famous Boston Strangler. However, cross-examination of Steve by sceptical psychiatrists led Bianchi to make some small but vital mistakes, and it emerged that Bianchi was deliberately faking Steve. Bianchi had read up on MPD, and Steve had been created to justify a plea of insanity, avoiding the death penalty.

But the differences between Bianchi and a real case of MPD are not as clear-cut as one might assume. The crucial difference is that Bianchi deliberately chose his alter, whereas in real MPD alters arise involuntarily, a way of coping with maltreatment. Yet there was a sense in which there truly were two Bianchis. The charmer was an attractive person, who lured many women into his bed prior to his becoming a rapist. The rape-murderer was cruel, hostile and violent. When he was the rapist, Bianchi did not think his evil self was someone else entirely, with a different name from Kenneth. But the two kinds of people were different. It is unlikely that, in moving between the personas, Bianchi was any more deliberate and voluntary than someone with MPD. Yes, he was very conscious in his creation of Steve when he needed a cover story, but no, he was not in control of whether he was Bianchi the charmer or Bianchi the rapist.

This may shed some light on the relationships of David Jones to Bowie and Ziggy. Jones chose Bowie as his stage name (based on the inventor of the knife of that name, an American folk hero). Gradually Jones came to see himself in most of his relationships as Bowie, although he always knew he was also Jones. When Bowie invented Ziggy, this was partly a deliberate commercial and artistic decision – much

like Bianchi's creating Steve for a practical purpose, a conscious act rather than one forced upon him by maltreatment
and done without awareness of what was happening. But it
seems from Bowie's account that he in time had periods of
being Ziggy during which neither Jones nor Bowie knew they
were being Ziggy. At such times, Jones could have been on
the road to MPD, with a loss of control of who was the host.

Although it might seem offensive as a comparison, in
terms of volition children's play is much like the different
Bianchis. The same could be said of the Jones–Bowie relationship. For a child the pretences involved in being a fairy
or a monster are largely spontaneously generated, coming
from the child's inner life, which in turn reflects parental care.
Bianchi's personas reflected his traumatic childhood: whether
he behaved like a charmer or a rapist would have been driven
by profound emotional needs just like those in children's play.
The same was true of Jones, Bowie and Ziggy.

NORMAL MULTIPLE PERSONAS

When Bianchi deliberately chose to pretend to have a Steve
personality, the psychological mechanisms would have been
very similar to the occasions when children deliberately invent
characters and choose to inhabit them. The best analysis of
the mechanics of such pretence comes from Shaun Nichols
and Stephen Stich*, who propose three mental components
through which the pretence is achieved: the *Possible World
Box*, the *UpDater*, and the *Script Elaborator*.

In the classic example, a child or adult pretending that
a banana is a telephone would add an initial premise to
their *Possible World Box* with the content 'This banana is a
telephone'. The *UpDater* then fills the *Possible World Box*

with other representations that follow from this fact, such as 'People can use this thing [the banana] to talk to other people who are far away.' The *Script Elaborator* adds other representations that do not directly follow from the initial premise but will make the pretence more complete. For example, it might add, 'This thing has buttons that can be pressed to make calls.'

As discussed in Chapter 5, a central problem of pretence is *quarantine*. Someone who is pretending that a banana is a telephone probably also believes that a banana cannot really be used to talk to other people who are far away. Representations of 'The thing in my hand is a telephone' and the 'The thing in my hand is a banana' are direct contradictions. As Nichols and Stich point out, 'If the mind's inference mechanisms treat both representations equally, they will arrive at a contradiction and produce inferential chaos: once a contradiction has been proved within a system, then anything can be proved.'

The *Possible World Box* schema resolves this problem. So long as the person marks the beliefs and places them into that quarantined zone of pretence, they are not treated as having the same meaning as in real life.

If we go back to Bianchi, it seems plausible that when he was pretending to be Steve, he was creating a *Possible World Box*, in exactly the same way as a child would when pretending to be a fairy or a monster. He invented a whole world of characteristics and activities for Steve that existed apart from Kenneth, and he then played out that character. (The same could be said of Jones, Bowie and Ziggy.) Using his *Script Elaborator* and *Updater*, Kenneth embellished Steve when confronted with detailed questioning by the psychiatrists. In passing off his Steve persona as a dissociated one about which Kenneth knew nothing, he made one seemingly small error when updating. A hostile psychiatrist pressed him to say what Steve's surname was. At first he blustered but, under pressure, he gave a name that turned out to be the same as one he had used fraudulently a few years earlier. When the police realised this, they had incontrovertible proof that Bianchi was faking. Had Steve been a true alter, he would not have made up a lie like that based on a previous act of deliberate fraud: he would either have known his surname or, if not, would have continued to say that he did not know: the addition of the surname was a blatantly self-serving attempt to sustain an illusion in order to avoid the death penalty.

The Nichols and Stich account of pretence provides a strong theoretical basis for the idea that it is not just people with MPD or children at play who have multiple personas – we all do. Nor do we have to formalise these personas by giving them different names, as Jones did in calling himself Bowie. This was explained well in a little-read essay by Stanley James*. He points out that it is normal for people to hold multiple contradictory positions, but one *Possible World Box* cannot contain all of them without chaos ensuing.

He starts with the example of a comedian he once heard doing impressions of celebrities. Unusually, this comedian would have the celebrities impersonating other celebrities. The comedian managed to convincingly impersonate Arnold Schwarzenegger impersonating Bill Clinton, or Michael Jackson doing Bob Dylan. I saw another example of this in an episode of *The Simpsons*: Harry Shearer, the actor who does the voice of 'Mr Burns', had Burns impersonating Elvis Presley.

Interestingly, Bowie did something very similar on his *Hunky Dory* album. As David Jones, he was adopting the persona of Bowie. Then, in one of the songs on the album, Bowie was singing in the style of Bob Dylan ('Song For Bob Dylan'). When playing, any of us might effortlessly engage in such multiple levels of pretence. Fiction is full of them: for example, the character Falstaff in Shakespeare's *Henry IV, Part 1*, when he impersonates someone else in the company of the king. Asked about Falstaff, Falstaff replies, 'the man I know. But to say I know more harm in him than in myself would be to say more than I know.'

James's point is that pretence can operate at more than one level at a time, and one *Possible World Box* would not be able to cope with the contradictions entailed. We have to propose further *Possible World Boxes* for each new level if logical meltdown is to be avoided.

James takes the amusing hypothetical example of a Russian spy working undercover in America. He is tired and would like to be at home but is invited to a party that it is critical he attend. There, he has to feign enthusiasm for the event and is forced to join in a game of charades. He is given the task of playing a dead cat, which he does by sprawling on the floor in a cat-like pose.

James points out that level upon level of pretence is required to do this, all of it perfectly feasible. First, the Russian spy is pretending to be an American, then he is pretending to enjoy the party, then he is pretending to be a dead cat. If all the representations required to accomplish this were placed into the one box, he would be having to believe he was a merry American who is also a dead cat. The simple solution is to suppose that more than one belief box is used to sustain the pyramid of pretence. By this means, it is perfectly possible for a person to believe two or more completely contradictory things.

Using the extreme example of people with split brains, a condition in which the corpus callosum – the tissue linking the two brain hemispheres – has been damaged, James shows how multiple beliefs can coexist. The left hemisphere of one man with this condition wanted to be a draughtsman, the right hemisphere a racing-car driver; also, his right hemisphere liked

President Nixon, but his left hemisphere disliked him. Another patient found his right hand undoing a shirt that had been selected for him and put on by his left hand. MPD provides similar proof of contradiction within the same brain: there can be sub-personalities with conflicting beliefs.

All of this raises a fundamental challenge to the idea that we have real/true and false selves. In fact, all of us have multiple selves, which are expressed to others through personas. Jones/ Bowie illustrates this in his professional and sexual relationships. Although he was exceptionally skilled in his manipulations, these are still indicative of the way most of us function.

EIGHT

'Tis a pity she was a whore: from the manipulator's sexploits to emotional health

Those who worked with Bowie and knew him well say that he was a curious mixture of warmth and ruthless self-interest: at least when young, he was a chameleon who changed his personality to suit whoever he was with.

Ken Pitt, who managed Bowie for a time and with whom he also lived, said that the 20-year-old Bowie 'had a way of sitting in a chair and looking at you with a certain intensity. He managed to look at you as though his eyes were slightly closed. But then you realised that they were in fact open and you got the impression that, as you were talking to him, he was analysing and dissecting every word you said and forming an opinion in his mind.' From this – possibly dissociated – position, his manipulative capacities were considerable. He had a talent for making people feel they had his whole attention – that they were the centre of his universe and were vital to his existence. They described having the odd feeling, when meeting him again after not having seen him for some time, that he had barely been able to function in their absence. In his company, people would report the giddy, tingly sensation usually felt when in love. Even hardened and sceptical journalists like Charles Shaar Murray, whose first love was possibly drugs and whose second was women, described having felt a kind of 'platonic man-love' for Bowie. One of Bowie's tricks was to pick words out of a person's sentences and repeat them, as if they had crystallised the thoughts in his own mind.

Combined with this capacity to charm was a finely judged ability to avoid upsetting colleagues he had rejected. He dropped musicians and managers without a backward look, yet they rarely felt animosity. He could keep professional balls in the air without dropping them, juggling different record company executives and managers. He knew how to be A Player.

A rare example of someone who was never wholly convinced by Bowie was Ian Hunter, the singer from the band Mott The Hoople. Even though he was taken up by Bowie with great enthusiasm and the band's version of Bowie's song 'All The Young Dudes' was a big hit, Hunter always remained suspicious. He said that Bowie 'could walk into the toilet one person and walk out another, and I never knew if it was just him putting on a little charade or if it was for real'. This was in 1972, before Bowie's cocaine period and the rapid shifts in personality that many reported. Hunter suspected that Bowie was hoping to learn from him how to have rapport with an audience: 'The type of thing that Mott had that he never had was humanity. I think he was upset because he never had riots. People were too polite to riot at his concerts. He sucks, like Dracula. He sucks what he can get and then he moves on to another victim.'

Even a passing acquaintanceship with Bowie's treatment of his fellow musicians suggests that there is some truth in this. He was quick to drop them when they had served his purpose and to move on. He was constantly on the lookout for new skills and ideas, and shameless in incorporating them into his work. One of his lovers, Ava Cherry, said, 'David had a tendency to control everyone around him. It was a mental control. Once he'd met them they would be his, he'd have them. He could make them do anything he wanted them to do.'

One exception was his manager, Tony Defries, with whom he had a contract between 1972 and 1982. A brilliant impresario, Defries used all the techniques of self-fulfilling prophecy to help Bowie become famous. During the early stages of the Ziggy Stardust project, he sold Bowie to Americans as successful in England and vice versa, at a time when he was truly successful in neither. Journalists in one nation were persuaded that he was 'happening' in the other, until both had publicised him so much that it became true. Defries's philosophy was that the way to become a star was to act like a star. To this end, he created a myth – partly based on reality – that Bowie hated any physical contact with strangers, and he hired an enormous bodyguard to keep them at bay. He also used Bowie's nervousness about flying to create mystique, so that Bowie had to take ocean liners to and from the US. There was accompanying pomp on his arrival at the docks, with, initially, manufactured crowds and press interest. Defries ensured that the tour entourage stayed only in the swankiest hotels, creating an aura of success, when in reality there was little money. He frequently claimed Bowie had sold millions of albums when he had only sold thousands. In short, Defries was a classic salesman who did a highly effective job.

However, he duped Bowie as well. Bowie paid a hefty price for getting into the same professional bed as such an unscrupulous man. Having barely read the contract in 1982, Bowie signed away all the rights to his music to a company controlled by Defries. When Bowie finally realised this, there was nothing he could do about it; his earnings for the period

1972–82 were nothing like what they could have been. It was not until he was free of the contract that Bowie became seriously wealthy, through *Let's Dance,* a highly commercial (but artistically unsatisfying) album and tour.

Once the penny did finally drop about Defries, in 1975, Bowie broke all personal contact with him, although there was nothing he could do to alter their commercial relationship. He had been cosseted by Defries's organisation, effectively mothered, with all his practical needs catered to; now he replaced Defries with Corinne Schwab. Completely loyal, she became his gatekeeper. There was even a period of two years during which his cousin Kristina was unable to make contact with him, owing to Schwab's control of access to Bowie.

If Bowie played fast and loose with his professional colleagues, it was little different in his personal life. Kristina was one of the very few people he remained close to for nearly all his life, and he would joke to her about how he would drop friends and lovers. 'We call them his *purges*', she said.

Bowie described his behaviour as 'terrible' when, as a young teen, he had first discovered the joys of girls. Following a school trip to Spain when he was 13, he was commemorated in the school magazine as 'Don Jones, the lover, last seen pursued by thirteen senoritas'. Jan Powling, a contemporary of his at school, described a date he had asked her out on. It is perhaps a testament to his charm even then that, years later, she seemed to bear no grudge when reporting that he had ended the date with her much prettier friend Deirdre on his arm – 'I don't blame David, she was one of the prettiest girls we knew.'

By the age of 17 he was in a band, and the other members remember him as having been 'obsessive' in his pursuit of women. Not only was he memorably good-looking, amusing and charming, he was also endowed with an exceptionally large penis, something that his friend and rival Marc Bolan always somewhat resented.

His treatment of women illustrates the power he had to enchant and make people feel good, as well as his ability to drop them without leaving a bad taste. It shows how fluid his personality was from the start, long before the fame or the drugs, and therefore how he must have been struggling for a sense of self, of identity.

Dana Gillespie (who was later to have some success as a singer herself) was 14 when she set her sights on him, describing herself as 'a very *forward* fourteen-year-old'. She managed to sneak into the dressing-room before a performance that the 17-year-old Bowie was giving at the Marquee Club in Soho. 'I was at a mirror brushing my hair and David came up and took the brush from my hand and carried on brushing, saying could he take me home that night, and I said "absolutely".' She was from an affluent home, and he used it as a port of call between tours. She recalls that as a lover he was 'determined, talented and *different* – he knew what he wanted, and he wanted to do well'.

He is scored equally highly by subsequent lovers, although he was very rarely sleeping with only one at a time. Natasha Korniloff was the costume and set designer for Lindsay Kemp in 1967. Bowie's affair with her began almost as soon as they met, and despite its messy ending, she still described him as 'a wonderful lover, absolutely without qualification, over anyone'. She found him quite incapable of doing anything for himself domestically, simply announcing he was hungry and expecting to be fed. Her enthusiasm for him years later is all the more surprising given that at the time she had no idea that Bowie was also Kemp's lover, and its discovery resulted in a nasty showdown between Kemp and Korniloff and a hysterical 'plea for help' act of self-harm by Kemp.

Soon after this fiasco, Bowie fell in love for the one and only time before, in his forties, he met his wife, Iman. Hermione Farthingale was a young middle-class singer and actress from South Kensington in London. They also met through Kemp, and Bowie soon moved into her attic flat. A relatively conventional person, she found his sexual demands excessive and was very disconcerted when she realised that he sometimes slept with men. When she ended the relationship after three months, Bowie commented that falling in love 'was an awful experience – it rotted me, drained me and it was a disease'. Her parents are thought to have disapproved of him, and although he did his best to win her back, it was to no avail. Until he met Iman, with the exception of his relationship with Hermione he proved himself incapable of giving himself to another person, of depending and being depended upon in a consistent and loving fashion for sustained periods.

For a brief period after the end of the Hermione affair, he was markedly effeminate. Bowie's colleagues in his band at the time were bothered by a gay patter that he sometimes used when speaking to them; they found it unsettling because they were confirmed heterosexuals. He would arrive at Ken Pitt's office, his (gay) manager, with his hair piled up in curls, exhibiting stagey feminine mannerisms, fluttering his eyelashes and flouncily crossing his legs when sitting down. However, within a short time he met Mary Finnigan, a journalist and single mother with two small children. She offered him a bed in her spare room, and within days he was sharing hers. As with other girlfriends, he was notable for his total lack of domesticity, happy to sit in a messy kitchen and expecting others to cook, clean and clear up. Just occasionally she would return home and find that he had cleaned the house from top to bottom, with a meal on the way, flowers and linen tablecloth set out, and providing live and recorded musical entertainment. Recalled Finnigan, 'I found his come-on very romantic and it was inevitable that love-making was part of it.'

Although appreciated by his lovers for his sexual imagination and empathy, Bowie often also relied on them for domestic support and a roof over his head. In this sense he was exploitative. One relationship that was suspiciously like a case of sleeping himself to the top was with record executive Calvin Mark Lee. Having known Lee for two years, Bowie started an affair with him only when he took a crucial job at Bowie's record company. Lee had to be philosophical about the relationships Bowie had simultaneously with women, including Hermione. (Lee was one of the men she felt uncomfortable about.) After Hermione rejected him, he moved in with Mary Finnigan. She knew nothing about his relationship with Lee, nor about that with his manager, Ken Pitt, and Pitt knew nothing about any of the others. Bowie was dividing himself up into separate boxes for all these men and women. The situation became even more complicated when Lee introduced Bowie to Angie, his bisexual future wife.

As Bowie put it, 'when I met Angie, we were both fucking the same bloke' (Lee). Finnigan got to know Bowie well and believes that Bowie never felt anything like the same interest in his male sexual partners: 'David was always more into women than men.' She maintained that his relationships with men were 'always more opportunist and contrived'. It is true that he enjoyed experimentation: with Angie: they would amuse themselves by dressing in clothes of the opposite sex and taking turns to act different gender roles during intercourse. If Finnigan had been uneasy with Bowie's requests to wear her clothes or make-up, it was meat and drink to Angie's sexual tastes. But while he and Angie sometimes engaged in threesomes, these were always with an additional female. For example, when Nita Bowes, an 18-year-old student, shared their house for a time, she joined them in their bed on half a dozen occasions.

Evidence of Bowie's primary heterosexual preference, and support for Finnigan's view that his primary interest was in women, comes from what happened once he became famous. During his first visit to Los Angeles in 1971, his record company promoter there reported that Bowie went into a sexual frenzy. 'He was grabbing girls right and left. He was picking up girls hitch-hiking in the street.' When Ziggy Stardust took off and Bowie was touring America in 1972–73, his renown made him a target for groupies. Stuey George, his bodyguard, had the job of selecting them: 'If he said "I need two chicks" or "I need five chicks" then I would try and arrange to get five chicks to spend the night with him.' While in Santa Monica on the 1972 tour, he visited a nightclub where there were several drag queens, who showed a strong interest. But when the man who had taken Bowie there was dancing with an attractive girl, Bowie walked onto the dance floor and asked if she was his girlfriend or his wife. Told she was neither, Bowie said, 'Well, I want her.' Having been introduced and after only a brief exchange, they disappeared into the bathroom.

On his second American tour in 1973, Bowie was even more sexually voracious. He would snap his fingers at the bodyguard and imperiously bark 'get me a drink, get me a girl', as if they were indistinguishable stimulants. Of course, in engaging in such behaviour he was little different from many rock stars or the musicians in his band, who were also all happy to sleep with groupies. Nor had Bowie lost his capacity to be a considerate lover, as Lori Matrix, then in her early teens, reported when she and her friend Sable spent a night with him. Having found their way into a restaurant where Bowie was eating, Sable was particularly eager to add him to her list of conquests, but it was Lori who was picked by the bodyguard. Lori insisted on taking Sable too.

After they had been ushered into the sitting-room area of his suite, Bowie emerged from the bedroom and took Lori into the bathroom, where a bubble bath awaited. He climbed in and asked her to wash his back. Lori recalled that 'he was sort of magnificent, this real pale creature sitting in the bath and I was really sort of turned on. He's talking to me and he's really intelligent, telling me things about himself, a real sensitive creature, and I didn't know what was going to happen and he stood up out of the bath and, ohhhhhhh, my God.' In awe of his big penis, she went with him into the bedroom, and, 'I'll never forget it, never, he was so gentle about the whole thing. Obviously whatever happened, happened, and we did it for about five or six hours. He was wonderful.'

What happened next is illuminating. Lori felt guilty that Sable was sitting neglected in the sitting room. On explaining this to Bowie, he responded that he only wanted to be with Lori. When she went to see Sable, she was naked beneath her coat and had inscribed 'I want to fuck David' in the moisture on the window. Lori returned to the bedroom and reiterated how much it meant to Sable, and, although he was reluctant, 'I brought her into the room. David was very good to her and gave her what she wanted and then we all fell asleep.'

Predatory or obliging, his behaviour continued to be highly promiscuous on the 1973 world tour. Returning on a train through Russia with Bowie, a journalist bluntly stated that 'He fucked everything that moved and quite a lot that didn't.'

Settled back in London with Angie and their 4-year-old son, life became hectic, but Bowie was still showing signs of sex addiction and of a need to boost himself through conquests. Pat Wadsley, recently hired as a junior publicist, was astonished when, having gone out to dinner with her and the family, he put his arm around her and suggested they go to his hotel. Feeling she had little choice in the matter – this was her new employer – she obliged and reported that he was 'very tender'. However, looking back on it, she believed he wanted her as a 'trophy', and that, at that time, having recently broken with Tony Defries, he wanted to use every means he could to feel in control of his staff. She could see no other explanation for his behaviour, because he did not repeat the exercise and at that time she was considerably overweight. She felt 'he was not overcome with lust' during the incident.

Although Angie maintained that she did not believe in monogamy and that both of them were free agents, there were relationships that did upset her. One was with Ava Cherry, an 18-year-old singer of African descent. At first she encouraged Ava to move in with them but soon became jealous, and Bowie had to set Cherry up in a separate flat nearby.

Cherry got used to his waywardness, although it upset her. She reported that what he wanted at that time were 'Black girls: any girls he would sleep with when I was with him were black. It was like "there's another one, what a gorgeous one, over there".' Stuey George would be asked to approach the ones he had picked out. Ava recalled that 'I couldn't stop him. I used to cry but he would always say "you can't fence me in". I was very faithful and he wanted me to be. He didn't have to be, but I had to be. He was a male chauvinist – but I liked it.'

It was not until 1990, when the 43-year-old Bowie met Iman, that he seems to have settled down. During his years in Berlin, between 1975 and 1978, he was as promiscuous as before: he enjoyed simply catching the eye of women in nightclubs as a way of summoning them.

As a personality-disordered man, at least until his forties, Bowie is not unusual in his manipulativeness. Indeed, there is evidence that as people age, they tend to become less personality-disordered. What is instructive is the way he seems to have managed to reach a healthier emotional state as he got older.

Having used Ziggy and other personas to console himself and escape madness, suicide and, eventually, drug addiction, Bowie seems to have gone into a period of depression. The three albums he produced while living in Berlin between 1975 and 1978 explored the despair he felt once he was no longer directly concerned with insanity. The first, *Low*, is especially troubled, with songs about the unhappy conclusion to his marriage to Angie and one whole side evoking black moods through purely instrumental pieces. However, once free of both Angie and his contract with Defries, Bowie does seem to have levelled out emotionally.

In 1982, Bowie produced *Let's Dance*, with an accompanying tour that made him a rich man, though few would maintain that it was a patch on the angst-driven work of the 1970s. It was designed to sell: a successful exercise in money-making. That his finest work was produced in an attempt to express his childhood adversities and to deal with his troubled personality supports the idea that great art tends to emerge from internal torment and conflict – although it seems clear that the best work is not produced during periods of actual mental illness.

Paul Mayersberg had been the scriptwriter for *The Man Who Fell To Earth* film and was well acquainted with the troubled Bowie of his cocaine era. Meeting him again when working on another film in 1982 (*Merry Christmas, Mr Lawrence*),

Mayersberg delivered this verdict on the new man that he met: 'The neurosis has largely left him or gone into another area of his life that I don't see. He doesn't seem quite as tense or hyper . . . He has become more physical rather than mental – health rather than disease has become interesting to him.'

Eight years later, Bowie met Iman, and they were both fulsome in their declaration of love for each other. Assuming these were true, they mean that he was finally able to depend on a woman – something he had avoided since the 'disease' of falling in love with Hermione Farthingale in 1969. From their meeting on, there were never any reports of infidelity. He and Iman married, and in 2000 they had a daughter, whom they called Alexandria. They lived between their houses in New York and Switzerland, and Bowie is said to have spent a good deal of time caring for his daughter, especially when she was small, before his heart attack in 2004.

At his mother's funeral in 2000, he met his Aunt Pat again for the first time in three decades. He embraced her, indicating forgiveness for the harsh words she had spoken about his treatment of Terry. He also appears to have had a good relationship with Duncan, his son by Angie, who has become a film director. Whether Bowie's relations with Angie following their savage divorce in the mid-1970s were civil is not known. At the time, using words worthy of Oscar Wilde's wit and savagery, he described her as 'having as much insight into the human condition as a walnut and a self-interest that would make Narcissus green with envy'.

I have no way of knowing whether Bowie had achieved a state of emotional health, an equilibrium, at the time of his death at the age of 69. That he still had sophisticated personas is illustrated by a story I was told by a man who had some dealings with him. After their meeting, the man could remember nothing at all of what Bowie had said. He mentioned this to Bowie's manager, who said, 'When speaking to people he does not know well, David has learnt to use words in such a way as to be unquotable.' This does not mean, however, that he had become an inscrutable recluse. He has said that 'There are about only half a dozen [friends] that I would think of as close in the accepted sense i.e. would I reach out to them in a time of real crisis?' He told Iman, 'All of them [his close friends] go back to my teenage years.' This suggests that in his last years he had made the transition back to David Jones from Bowie, via Ziggy, and the other personas that followed.

That Bowie may have achieved a state of peace is indicated by his comment about what was arguably his greatest single musical composition, the song 'Heroes', released in 1980. He said the song 'was about compassion, facing reality and standing up to it and deriving some joy from the very simple pleasure of being alive. Through love, in partnership with others, destiny can be achieved.'

Let us assume, for a moment, that Bowie had become emotionally healthy. (I have set out in more detail what I mean by that in my book *How to Develop Emotional Health**.) What, in particular, would we mean by the idea that he developed authenticity? Given the questions raised in chapter 7 about the validity of the notion of a unitary, true self, what would authenticity entail?

It is commonly assumed that, along with our true self, we have many false ones that we present to the world. The assumption is that the true self lies behind these masks. It is not really quite that simple. We do, of course, find ourselves often in the position of feeling and thinking one thing but presenting a different front to the world. We tell others that we are fine when feeling the opposite, or we tell our children their painting is wonderful when it is not. But that does not mean we have a single true self, nor are the masks that we adopt simply false.

What seems true to us in one context may not be so in another. Consider this startling example of an experiment in which 35 heterosexual young men were asked about their sexual preferences*. Presented with 16 potential sexual partners, the men did not think they would be attracted towards many of them, including 12-year-old girls, animals or other men and women in their sixties. They would not ply potential mates with alcohol to make it easier to get sex, nor would they slip drugs into their drinks to make them defenceless against sexual advances. If a woman said 'no' to an advance, they would respect that.

However, the following day the same men were placed in separate rooms, shown sexually arousing pictures and asked to masturbate themselves close to orgasm. Just before ejaculation, they were told to cease and to answer the same raft of questions as on the previous day. Their answers were significantly different. Now, the appeal of sex with a 12-year-old girl, with someone extremely fat, with someone they hated, watching a woman urinate, an animal, all these and more, were much greater. In fact, close to the point of climax, the only things they would not consider were sex with the lights on and with another man. What was more, they were significantly more likely to urge drink on a potential female partner to make her vulnerable, to slip a drug into her drink and to pressurise her after she had said no.

Which was the true self of each man on the two different days? On the first day he had one set of predilections, on the second day it was the opposite, but it was still the same man. The one who said he did not feel desire for an extremely fat woman or for an animal was being true to himself, as was the aroused one who said he did desire them. What is true of us in one circumstance can be false in another. This seems like powerful evidence that we can have more than one true self.

Psychologists have laid great store on the idea that there is a 'Big-5' collection of personality traits, which are fixed for all of us: varying degrees of openness to experience, conscientiousness, extroversion, agreeableness and neuroticism. For decades, establishment psychology has asserted that our particular mixture remains stable through time, in all situations and social roles. To this day, students are taught that our unique cocktail of these traits is largely anchored in our genes, despite the complete absence of any genes having been shown to strongly influence them*.

In fact, our traits vary considerably, depending on context*. I may be open to experience when going to see a new film but cagey and cautious if I meet a new boss. I may be the epitome of extroversion when enjoying the launch of one of my books but inhibited and shy if meeting a powerful potential employer. What is more, personalities can change over time – the timid child can become the daring adult; following divorce from her overbearing husband, the neurotic wife can become a calm and stable woman.

It is true that people who fluctuate wildly in their personality are often also distressed. Such instability seems to reflect a lack of a solid sense of self, feeling, instead, fragmented and chaotic.

It is also true that people who are prone to being engulfed by roles and social situations, always adapting to them and losing track of who they are, end up feeling false and hologrammatic. A person who constantly remoulds the self in line with social demands lacks integrity and self-direction. People who feel there is a gap between what they say they are really like and the person they are required to be in their social roles (wife, employee, caring friend) describe feelings of frustration and unreality in consequence.

The implication might be that it is best to be the same person in all contexts. Yet that is hardly feasible, as we saw in chapter 7. From early teenage onwards, we realise that it is essential to develop varying selves. While there are people who aspire to the unitary ideal, it runs the risk of a maladaptive rigidity and inflexibility. To be always extrovert is not advisable. To be true to your neuroticism in all situations, displaying and openly admitting your insecurities or phobias or depressed mood, is unlikely to be an effective prescription for professional or personal success. Indeed, one of the signs of neuroticism is that it is beyond one's control, an incapacity to adapt to situations that might require one to conceal something – one over-shares, giving more information than others need.

Richard Ryan and colleagues maintain that integration is defined not as being consistently the same person in all contexts, but, rather, as feeling authentic*. Ryan's authenticity refers to experience authored by the self and caused internally. People feel most authentic when they act with a full sense of choice and self-expression. These entail the ability to effectively regulate and maintain one's intentional states, to process new information more deeply and to think more creatively. Defined like that, felt authenticity is a better indicator of integration and organisation than exhibiting the same traits in all settings.

To effectively express ourselves, we must manifest different behavioural styles in different roles, be inconsistent in our traits. It is not differentiation or variation in our personality traits, *per se*, that is indicative of fragmentation in personality but, rather, betrayal of the feeling of self-determination that underpins authenticity.

In the decisive test of this theory, students were asked to measure their Big-5 traits in five different roles: student, employee, child, friend and romantic partner*. The students' levels of authenticity and their well-being in each role was also measured. Sure enough, the results showed considerable and consistent variability in Big-5 traits according to roles. The students reported being most extroverted in the friend role, most neurotic in the student role, most conscientious in the employee role, most open to experience in the romantic partner role and least agreeable in student and child roles. The idea that we are the same person in all situations, with the same personality traits, was disproved. Who the students were depended on roles, not on some inbuilt set of invariant traits.

It is true that those who reported more similar traits across roles also described themselves as feeling more autonomous and authentic. They were the most satisfied and least distressed. This suggests that a measure of self-consistency, of being the same person in different situations, is indeed 'a good thing'. But consistency only conferred well-being if it was accompanied by a sense of autonomy and authenticity.

The finding contradicts the postmodern claim that in our complex society it is best to accept that you must simply have many different selves, with no *internal* consistency across contexts. We must, indeed, behave differently in different contexts, but that does not mean we do not have an inner truth that spans them. In other words, neither the 'unitary, true self' story – in which we are only true if we are the same in all contexts – is right, nor is the post-modern tale of no authentic self.

In the face of their own internal chaos, too many authors have thrown up their hands, perhaps because they themselves are in pieces, personally, and have pressed the Hyperspace button of total existential relativity. The Hyperspace button was the one you could use to escape when about to be obliterated in the *Space Invaders* computer game so popular in the 1980s: it was the last resort, one that might give you a second chance but usually ended in your destruction. The relativistic, post-modern authors of too many books, cultural studies essays, newspaper articles and broadcast programmes are just individuals who have lost the plot. In trying to spread their confusion and to maintain that it has a scientific or philosophical basis, they are seeking to reassure themselves and to excrete their confusion by creating it in others.

What remains constant in our diverse and multiple lives is not acting the same in all contexts, as the Big-5 theorists maintain. Rather, that thread is the sense of authenticity – autonomy and self-determination. This derives from our childhood history*. Our family politics and individual care in the early years becomes etched into our brains. Patterns of early experience cause us to have consistent patterns of brainwaves and levels of different chemicals. They even affect the size of different parts of our brain. Each of us has unique patterns of electro-chemistry that reflect our individual experience. This is what feels authentic to us, even if that experience was of severe maltreatment.

What the relativists ignore is the way their personal confusion dates back to their childhood. Recalling this and relating it to who we present ourselves as in different settings is the clue to the exit offered by David Bowie's work and life: persona therapy.

NINE

Upping Your Ziggy:
persona therapy
and the power of pretence

Bowie managed to gain control of which host was in charge of his personas, but for many of us that is not something we are used to doing. There are also some notable examples of famous people who allowed destructive personas to take hold.

I have in my possession an audiotape of John Hinckley, the man who tried to assassinate Ronald Reagan, speaking on the telephone to Jody Foster, the actress. Foster was at university at the time, and it is clear from the exchange that Hinckley believes himself to be Foster's boyfriend, even though he had never met her. Hinckley went on to shoot Reagan as a proof of his love for her. He had developed a fully delusional boyfriend persona in which the divide between pretence and the real had broken down.

I also have dozens of audiotapes of Mark Chapman, the man who killed John Lennon, explaining the assassination to psychologists and psychiatrists. (These resulted in a TV programme available on the Internet*.) Chapman was not delusional, but he did strongly identify with Holden Caulfield, the central character of Salinger's *The Catcher in the Rye*. In 1980, Chapman sincerely believed that Lennon had betrayed his fans by maintaining that he had grown up and put his 'childish' past ideas behind him. Identified with Caulfield, Chapman was depressed about the state of the world and felt that the transition from childhood to adulthood entailed becoming 'phoney'. Shooting Lennon was his attempt to publicise this idea. When he was arrested, a copy of *The Catcher in the Rye* was found in his possession, with the words 'This is my statement' written on the inside cover: the book, which uses the word 'phoney' 108 times, was Chapman's explanation for his terrible crime.

After his capture, Chapman was repeatedly asked whether he believed himself to actually be Caulfield, but he always denied this, showing no signs of believing himself to be his fictional hero. In characterising himself as 'the catcher in the rye of my generation', he was grandiose. But the pretend–real distinction had not broken down. What is more, there were nuggets of truth in his beliefs – the innocence of children is real, as is the relative falsehood of many adults.

The key to authentic adulthood is having personas that express self-determination. Bowie's use of personas offers all of us clues to ways of realising our potential through them.

You may recall that in Chapter 5 I mentioned my son's penchant for being Nibbles The Squirrel and how useful that persona could be to him. I had a startling example of this when, aged 9, he was invited for a trial to join the academy of the Premiership club with whom he had been training for two years. We had to travel some distance, and during the ride my son focused on being in what he called Happy Land, a world of magical elves, in which Nibbles The Squirrel sometimes frolicked. As we approached our destination, he was in a mood of pure sunshine, merrily babbling about what Nibbles was getting up to.

I had played down the extent to which this was a 'do-or-die' one-off opportunity for him to shine, although it probably was. I did not want him to be tense or to feel under pressure to succeed: this was to be just an interesting experience for him. He had previously worked out when going to normal games where he wanted to perform well that it was best for him to visit Happy Land on the way there. During his early football 'career', he had enjoyed listening to high-energy rock songs to get him into an atavistic state, songs like 'Dynamite' (Taio Cruz), 'All Along The Watchtower' (Jimi Hendrix) and 'Rebel Rebel' (Bowie). This would put him into 'search and destroy' mode. For example, sometimes, while playing as goalkeeper, he would dribble up the whole pitch past all the six opposing players. However, since turning 8, he had worked out that it was better for him to be more calm and engaged with his fantasy world during the journeys to games. (This was nothing to do with me: I preferred listening to Hendrix.)

Shortly before our arrival at the training ground, I was a bit worried that he might be too relaxed. Perhaps the stress of knowing that he was about to play against some of the best boys of his age in the country was making him travel too far into Happy Land, overcompensating for the anxiety of being put to the test. Hoping to focus him a little, I suggested he concentrate for a moment on two things that he should try to do in the game that day – dominate and pass – but he did not seem to be listening. He just nodded, then went back to muttering about how wizards were playing with his magic elves.

Standing behind the wire fence where the parents were corralled, I was stunned by his performance. It was the best I had seen from him, and he was at least the equal of the most accomplished boys he was competing with. Afterwards, as we walked to the car, I could see he was lit up, his face wreathed in smiles, having enjoyed himself. In the car, I told him I could hardly believe what I had just seen: that he had played superbly, it had seemed so easy, how he could be as good as the best. He agreed, and we spent some time squeaking in Nibbles mode. When we had calmed down, I asked what had been on his mind during the games (there were two). He said, 'I didn't have any thoughts, I was just thinking of nothing at all, nothing at all. *I just imagined this was a normal game.* I did think when we got to half-time, "my god, how did I do that?" But I stopped thinking about it and just went on playing.'

This was an odd answer, in that he was all too visibly deliberate in the way he played. When in defence, he was stopping the attackers with unusual zest and cunning, then passing the ball out to his own team, not dribbling too much (his particular talent). In attack, he was also playing with far more awareness of other players than usual. In scoring a goal, he did it with a style and ease that was startling. If he was treating it as a normal game, how come he was playing so abnormally well?

It emerged from further discussion that what he had done was to simply ignore the possibility that he was being judged. Whereas the other players – whether already part of the Premiership team or not – seemed very on edge, he did not. If he made mistakes, it did not bother him, he just got stuck in. This 'I am playing in a normal game' part of him inoculated against fear of failure.

Yet, running alongside this self, it emerged, there was another one, which was acutely aware of the need to play harder and better than usual. It seemed to instruct him in how to adapt to the higher standard, even causing him to be very vocal in calling for the ball or warning teammates of dangers, when normally he was silent. He explained that he sometimes called for the ball to put his teammates in a bad light if they failed, since they were also his rivals.

Here is an example of how using different personas and selves can hugely benefit us. In the car, instead of listening to my pompous injunctions, he emigrated from his anxieties to Happy Land. Through his Nibbles persona and associated pretences, he entered a highly relaxed state. Doubtless his cortisol levels (the fight–flight hormone) were at the 'calm' setting when he got out of the car.

Once the game began, he used a mixture of two simultaneously operating personas to regulate his experience and performance. At its heart was what, in other contexts, might be seen as a delusion. Part of him truly believed himself to be in a situation where there was no pressure to succeed, no people to please – just a normal game for his usual team of that time, where he was among the best performers. The story nicely illustrates the idea that we need multiple *Possible World Boxes* to avoid contamination between different personas when engaged in pretence. In one box, he saw himself as in a normal game, pretending that this was not a trial at all. In another box he pictured himself as a Vlad The Impaler, a rampant Mongol laying waste to dangerously skilled opponents. Using the two boxes, he could operate the two pretences simultaneously, without any sense of self-contradiction. Paradoxically, both personas were true.

Conventional sports psychology does not formulate what my son was doing in terms of personas, but there is, in fact, a strong body of evidence to support the power of illusions in sporting and other fields. Hundreds of studies have demonstrated this for placebo pills*: that if you give tablets containing chalk to one group and pills that contain an active ingredient to another group, the chalk tablets can work just as well (placebo = 'I will please' in Latin). Three quarters of the effect of antidepressant pills is based on the belief that they will work*. In the realm of sport, there is evidence that imagining that there is a God who can be called upon through prayer for protection or to enhance performance is an effective strategy*. In my terms, doing so is creating an illusory omnipotent persona (which is experienced as external and separate from you) who watches over another part of yourself, the part that is trying to win.

Without invoking any deities, sports psychologists routinely teach positive thinking and the elimination of the negative. This creates potential contradictions. At one level, sportsmen may believe that they are best and that they will win; at another level, they do know that this is not necessarily true. That is dealt with in the way my son did, by switching between personas in their different boxes. As the golfer Nick Faldo put it, he has to use hyper-realistic calculations to decide which shot to play with which club, but, having done so, 'you have to flick the mental switch and execute the shot as if there was never any doubt that you would nail it'*.

The practical implication is that we can achieve a measure of volition, of choice, through finding the right persona or mixture thereof. Some psychologists would call this 'reframing': re-presenting a situation or an aspect of our behaviour in a different way. What I am talking about is something far more radical that can be done on our own. Having identified who we need to be, we can enter those personas simultaneously.

For example, the teenage daughter of a friend of ours was consistently top in her class at school. In classroom exams she excelled. However, at the end of every summer in this large school, there was a practice session for the conditions of GCSE: the girls had to sit papers in a large gymnasium, mimicking the conditions that would be encountered when the national exam was taken. Under these conditions, her performance was far poorer.

Her teacher made a suggestion: that when she was doing the real GCSE, she should pretend to herself that she was simply sitting in her classroom doing the test as normal. Sure enough, through that pretence she was able to excel in her GCSEs when they came along.

For all of us, it is valuable to write down a list of the different personas we have and give them names. I have many. At the time of writing I am engaged in a lot of different professional activities: producing this book, but also seeing clients and giving talks of various different kinds (some to the general public, some to commercial or professional organisations) on diverse subjects relating to different books I have written, along with various kinds of equally diverse media activities, from writing newspaper articles to appearing on radio or TV. I daresay you also have a busy life with lots of different professional commitments, whether you work freelance or in an organisation. Even if you work as a checkout operative in a supermarket, there are quite a few different personas required for that job.

As well as my professional life, there is my domestic one. The many extracurricular activities of a 14-year-old daughter and an 11-year-old son entail contact with various professionals and numerous other parents. There is our social life, which does not get any less complex for my getting older – I have long-standing intimates dating back to childhood but also numerous more recent friends and acquaintances. All these activities demand that I adapt my persona. I try to be aware of those open to me and of how my personal history relates to them.

It is highly beneficial for us to understand that we do not have a single 'true' self – our family histories create the potential for many different ones – and that we can have a measure of choice about which ones host our conscious lives at any given time. However, simply knowing this may not be sufficient for us to resolve enduring problems.

There are several forms of therapy that start from the premise that we are many people – most notably ego state therapy* and parts therapy*. These offer various ways to analyse one's current emotional state and to survey the selves one has available.

In my work with clients, I explain early on Eric Berne's concept* that we can all be in any one of three modes at any point in time: parent, adult or child (known as PAC):

Parent mode: in which you mimic your parents;

Adult mode: in which you are able to be relatively detached from emotion, seeking an objective view of the situation you are in;

Child mode: in which you are in the grip of how it was for you when small, reliving that, even though you are now grown up.

More than any other single model, I find that clients can instantly relate to PAC and apply it. Being in Parent or Child mode is not always 'wrong': indeed, when it is the angels in the nursery that are pulling the strings, they are benign. But most of us can grasp that when things are going wrong, the Adult mode is very helpful.

PAC is just the beginning. As our work proceeds, we discuss the way the client was cared for in childhood and what preceded that. We run through chronologically, starting with what they know of their grandparents, on through their parents' history and into the clients' childhood.

Sooner or later, a narrative emerges of where this person came from and who they were required to be in their original family. At that point, I write them a letter, summarising this as best I can, and they can correct any misapprehensions. We use this narrative in order to make sense of the many people that begin to come to light as they describe their contempo-rary selves. Slowly, in bits and pieces, different selves emerge through the mists of the childhood and their contemporary life (which may be a war zone that interrupts our exploration of the past and has to be accommodated). As we go along, we connect up the different people they had to be as children with the personas they currently possess.

For example, when I first started working with Olga, it was as if different people were turning up to each session, and also switching from one to another during them. Occa-sionally she was reasoned and calm – what we came to call Professional Olga. Mostly, she was Toddler Olga, a torrent of emotion, frequently tearful and flooded by anger or fear.

Aged 37, she lived alone and was plagued by remorse about her unsatisfactory past love affairs, mostly with mar-ried men: Rejected Olga. Still frozen at a 6- or 7-year-old pre-sexual stage, Cinderella Olga hoped a knight in shining armour was going to save her. Speaking very rapidly, she would burst into my office like a vortex. We came to speak of this period in our work as The Tsunami.

Over time, she was able to tell me about the constant war-ring between her parents, including blows from her often hys-terical and always furious and terrifying, yet fearful, mother, with her father retreating into an affair and his work, when not screaming back at her. As well as witnessing this dishar-mony and violence, threats of divorce were a weekly occur-rence, creating great insecurity that the household could be broken up at any time.

Olga was the second of five children, and when not being severely neglected, she was stigmatised as chubby by her mother, with food becoming a major issue. From her teens onwards, there were bouts of bulimia, of semi-starvation or overeating. Her mother frequently hit her, as did her older sister. On one occasion, with her sister's boot on her head against a stone floor, Olga had believed she was about to die. Horses and dogs were her only friends and family during an exceptionally lonely childhood spent in the middle of the countryside. During holidays she spent most of her time in the stables.

She was shamed into feeling that her body was disgusting. As she entered puberty, her mother falsely claimed that her father's attitude to her was lascivious; she was envious of Olga's nubility and made it shameful. She forced Olga to attend teenage parties dressed in inappropriate clothes – ones her mother had worn in the 1970s – as if taken from a children's dressing-up cupboard.

Ashamed of her attractiveness, Olga sought her father's attention by being an assiduous student. In therapy, she was very capable and was able to make rapid use of my support, creating artworks and written summaries to profile her different personas. Although at first rather cerebral – her intellect and emotional life were stored in separate boxes – she gradually linked conceptual models to her true feelings. Rather than speaking of personas, she developed the idea that there were different radio stations in her head – mostly narratives from her mother: Radio Food, Radio Fat, Radio Blame and so on. They would tell her what a failure she was for being childless and single, overweight (even when she was not) and worthless.

Olga quickly formed a strong attachment to me. At first we had daily meetings, moving gradually to twice a week, with her sending me emails two or three times a day. She did not require me to reply in detail or at length, just to acknowledge them with an encouraging comment or two.

After only four months, Olga calmed down considerably. The turning point was when we addressed her constant battle with food by analysing meal times on a typical day during her childhood. What that uncovered was Refugee Olga.

Olga's mother was raised in Eastern Europe during the Second World War. At the age of 4, following the Russian liberation of her country from the Germans, she was sent to live with an aunt for six years. For most of her early years, food was very scarce. This led to a constant sense in her mother that severe privation was always just around the corner.

That translated into an eccentric pattern of cooking and meals on Olga's mother's part. She would put some meat into the oven to cook overnight and then expect her children to eat large quantities of this dried-out, not very appetising breakfast, along with copious amounts of porridge. The children were pressured to eat so much of this unexciting combination that it often left them, and especially Olga, feeling sick. No sugar, salt or oil were permitted – it was a scorched-earth diet. The usual variety of foods available to an affluent family in late 1980s Britain was not provided. Instead of eggs, toast, cereal or fruit juice, the fare was accompanied by lavish trimmings of resentment from her mother, with which she reacted to even the simplest of requests for Olga's needs to be met.

The wolfing down of the eccentric breakfast combination was required because no lunch was provided. Olga must stock up, because that was all she would get until the evening – much as it had been for her mother as a girl. During the day, she had to scavenge for food, finding what apples or berries she could during the summer, or what she could find in the larder if a chance arose to sneak into the kitchen. Supper was bizarre: her father would be cooked a standard meat with two vegetables, but the children would still be on the strange rations of breakfast time. Most evenings, a savage row would break out between her parents; sometimes they came to blows. Olga could not recall any time when her parents had held hands and seemed loving, and there was no sign that they had a sex life. They slept in separate bedrooms from when she was aged 11.

For school, Olga would be supplied with curious mixtures of food types for her packed lunch, like some roasted meat and a random kiwi fruit. This combination made her a laughing stock, and she became ashamed to eat it in public.

On top of this, Olga's mother fanatically supervised food intake, even when she was not present. If Olga went to visit one of her few friends or to stay with her aunt, strict injunctions were imposed as to what she could consume. Her mother would telephone whoever was in charge to check that these rules were being obeyed. Consequently, Olga's relationship with food became boom and bust. When at her grandmother's, if Olga found a six-pack of KitKats, she would gobble the whole lot in one sitting before anyone could stop her.

What became apparent in the single session in which all this emerged was that Olga's mother had imposed the harsh conditions of her own early years. If there was food, eat it up quickly before someone took it; stock up for the coming scarcity.

Olga insightfully pointed out that her mother had conflated love with food to an exceptional extent, because she had not understood that the core trauma for her had been being sent to stay with her aunt at the age of 4. Instead of understanding that this had led to a severe sense of loss, a hunger for her mother's love, Olga's mother had equated her mother's absence with a lack of food. In accord with this, there is strong evidence that prolonged separation from parents when small during the Second World War was still affecting its victims 60 years later*.

Once Refugee Olga was uncovered, Adult Olga was liberated from her daily food torment. Prior to this, living alone, she had spent hours monitoring her food intake (as if her mother might telephone and demand to know what had been eaten) and being sporadically overwhelmed by the urge to consume large quantities of creamy, oily, and salty foods. Her mother had very systematically trained her to regard food as scarce. Although this had long since ceased to be true, when alone in her home, she would be assailed by the need to consume.

What was more, through her relationship with me, Olga ceased to fear rejection. She felt accepted, not judged, and that someone was benignly interested in her welfare. Using that as a platform, she was able to plug into her social network, and, no longer terrified of rejection or drawn to married men or to ones as needy or conflict-ridden as her former self, she become proactive in seeking out potential mates. Radio Mum was largely silenced, no longer providing a commentary that she was fat, stupid, uninteresting and worthless. Now able to take the advice of a sensible friend, having distanced herself from a variety of ex-friends who had wallowed in her difficulties, as her mother had, she joined an upmarket dating site. Given that there are four female graduates for every three males, there is an increasing scarcity of compatible men for single women as they enter their thirties, so this was a sensible decision by Adult Olga*.

Olga's story illustrates what can be achieved, in this case in a short period, by developing a dialogue within oneself between the different voices that stay with us from childhood and are expressed in personas. In the extreme, as described so well by Eleanor Longden*, the voices (or auditory hallucinations) are outside the head, but where they are internal, the principle of such dialogue is the same in the majority of us. Having begun that debate, it becomes possible to take charge, to decide upon a new host for our multiple selves.

One might call that the Core Persona. Core Olga, for example, was a calm, emotionally engaged woman who was able to tap into the positives that she had developed both during and after her childhood, like her intellect and artistic creativity.

The finding that genes seem to play little part in explaining why, psychologically, we are (or are not) like our parents, or siblings are different (or similar), has momentous implications. Although we cannot change the colour of our eyes by merely wishing it so, we can change who we are through our minds. The idea that personas can do this is David Bowie's legacy to us.

It was the difference in their childhood experiences that explained why Bowie was chosen for greatness and Terry became suicidally mad. To some extent, this theory merely replaces genetic determinism with another kind, nurturism. The fact that sexual abuse in childhood hampers the growth of key parts of the brain suggests the possibility that maltreatment can cause irreversible limits to who you can be. While it may emerge that talking therapies or drugs can cause those parts of the brain to grow, it seems likely that our early years do create the parameters of our destiny.

But there seems to be considerable flexibility within those parameters. Whether the severely maltreated, like Terry, end up throwing themselves under a train or, instead, become relatively emotionally healthy seems to depend on a lot of factors, beyond the early years. Meeting the right partner, friend or therapist can profoundly alter the trajectory. While it may have been written in the detail of Terry's maltreatment that he would never be able to express himself and find self-determination to the extent that Bowie did, there are huge variations in how maltreatment plays out.

The implication of Bowie's life and work is that we do have a choice in who we are. Personas are a key means by which to exercise it. When you finish reading this sentence, consider who you want to be: start hosting your life. Up your Ziggy.

NOTES

Introduction

xv **the TED talk by Eleanor Longden:** www.ted.com/talks/eleanor_longden_the_voices_in_my_head

Chapter 1

2 **highly questionable edifice of psychiatric symptoms:** Kraepelin, 2012.

2 **the biological aspects of mental illness:** Klerman, 1978.

2 *Diagnostic and Statistical Manual of Mental Disorders* (*DSM-5*): APA, 2013.

3 **its supposed boundary to breaking point:** All the statements in the succeeding three paragraphs are supported by studies reported in Bentall, 2004.

5 **far greater than that of the schizophrenic:** Laing & Esterson, 1970.

6 **was entitled *The Divided Self*:** Laing, 1960.

8 **connotations of Terry:** Gillman & Gillman, 1987, noted the close similarity between Terry and the painting of a young man by Ernst Haeckel, which was used by Bowie as the model for the cover for Iggy's album *Lust For Life*. Iggy was portrayed on the cover much like the young man in the painting, who had been a friend of the painter and had gone mad.

12 **the subject of conversation is emotionally charged:** Bentall, 2004.

Chapter 2

21 **schizophrenics are at greater risk of suffering themselves:** Mortenson et al., 1999.

22 **this has negative consequences:** Read & Dillon, 2013, chap. 12.

22 **transmission is through nurture, not nature:** James, 2014b.

22 **have been demonstrated to play a significant role:** James, 2014b.

22 **believe that genes still will be found:** Plomin & Simpson, 2013.

Notes

22   **can explain only 1–5% of the risk:** Plomin & Simpson, 2013.

22   **identikits will not have the illness:** Bentall, 2004.

23   **about schizophrenia goes for bipolar disorder:** Plomin & Simpson, 2013.

23   **was published in 2012:** Varese et al., 2012.

23   **the relationship of childhood adversity to schizophrenia:** Matheson et al., 2012.

23   **As the number of adversities rises, so does the risk:** John Read, one of the authors of the analysis of 41 studies (Varese et al., 2012), has explored these and other related findings in greater detail (Read & Dillon, 2013, chap. 18). He pointed out that the more extreme the childhood adversity, the greater the risk of adult psychosis. This strongly suggests a causal relationship between adversity and psychosis – that adversity almost certainly is a cause of psychosis. What is more, the type of adversity matters, and the most recent evidence suggests that specific kinds of maltreatment lead to specific kinds of psychotic symptoms (Ajnakina et al., 2016).

Read deals with the common objections made to this evidence. He points out that it need not entail blame to implicate parental care in causing psychosis, it is a matter of understanding how it comes about. Some of the studies are based on adult memories of childhood, and it has been objected that not only can this not be trusted, but that this is especially so for the recall of 'mad' people. But there is good evidence suggesting that the memories of the psychotic are, by and large, accurate over a seven-year period (Fisher et al., 2011). Read also shows that the evidence cannot be dismissed on the grounds that only those with a genetic predisposition develop psychosis as a consequence of childhood adversity. Recent evidence shows that when the psychosis of parents is allowed for, it is the maltreatment that puts children at greater risk of becoming psychotic, not the fact that psychosis runs in the family (Wigman et al., 2012). Nor does the argument stand up that adult psychotics were difficult children, and this had caused parents to maltreat them.

23   **more likely to be psychotic than if you had suffered none:** Shevlin et al., 2008.

23   **each kind of maltreatment has also been analysed:** A review of 59 studies found that 47% of women diagnosed as psychotic suffered sexual abuse, and 29% of men Symptoms are more likely if there has been incest rather than abuse by someone outside the nuclear family; repeated penetrative incestuous rape is most harmful (Read et al., 2008.)

Half of the psychotics had been physically abused. The majority of abusers were family members, particularly fathers. The earlier the abuse occurs, the greater the risk. For example, a large study of British children showed that they were 2.4 times more likely to exhibit psychotic symp-

166

toms at age 12 if physically abused after age 7, but 3.5 times more likely if the abuse started before that (Read & Dillon, 2013).

Emotional abuse seems to be even more damaging than sexual and physical abuse. An Italian study showed that those emotionally abused as children were 12 times more likely to be schizophrenic than the general population. The sexually abused in this sample were only twice as likely to be schizophrenic, the physically abused 6 times as likely. An American study followed adolescents for 15 years and found that over one third became schizophrenic if both parents had been hostile, critical and intrusive, compared with none where only one or neither parent had been. Other studies find that if parents are overprotective, or if they are very controlling but without showing love, this raises the risk.

Emotional and physical neglect, more than parental loss, are also common in the childhoods of schizophrenics. There is some evidence that parental separation may be more of a risk factor than the death of a parent: the rising divorce and separation rates of the last 50 years may have contributed considerably to the creation of psychosis.

23 **increasing the risk twelvefold:** Read & Dillon, 2013, chap. 18.

24 **were widely read in the 1960s:** Laing & Esterson, 1970.

24 **a weak sense of self in infants and toddlers:** Khan, 1963; Kohut, 1978.

24 **if care before age 2 has been poor:** Dutra et al., 2009; Ogawa et al., 1997.

24 **resulting from inadequate care, and later schizophrenia:** Alexander et al., 1998; Pickering et al., 2008; Read & Gumley, 2008.

24 **has also been implicated in psychosis:** Cannon et al., 2003.

24 **to have a schizophrenic offspring:** Gottesman, 1992, p. 99.

25 **Human Genome Project findings make this improbable:** James, 2014b.

25 **love and security that under-3s need:** Snellen et al., 1999.

25 **specific maltreatments have specific outcomes:** Read (Read & Dillon, 2013, chap. 18) shows that the content of symptoms has meaning. The precise contents of severely maltreated children's hallucinations reflect the kind of adversity suffered. For example, physical or sexual abuse, neglect and so on may be directly mirrored by what the child (and later adult) hallucinates. When people have delusions, it seems that they are reliving bad past experiences or remembering them, albeit through hallucinations or ideas that seem crazy when taken out of context.

26 **dangerous situations and relationships:** Read & Dillon, 2013, chap. 18. Childhood adversities cause children to grow up to become adolescents and adults who put themselves in danger of further maltreatment – 'revictimisation'. The majority of psychiatric patients had been physically assaulted as adults, as well as as children. More than half of women

sexually abused as children go on to be sexually assaulted as adults. It seems that childhood adversity leads people towards risky adult behaviour. Hence, although there is little doubt that use of strong hallucinogens, like skunk cannabis, increases the risk of psychosis (Di Forti et al., 2009), it is also the case that cannabis users are much more likely to have suffered childhood adversity (Konings et al., 2012). They use the drug to self-medicate the distress caused by the childhood maltreatment. The further problems created by risky behaviour increase the risk of psychosis.

26 **In a recent review of the evidence:** Read et al., 2014.

26 **the brain and the patterns of brainwaves:** In particular, there is strong evidence that the early maltreatment affects the growth of different parts of the brain. For example, a woman who was sexually abused as a child has 5% less of the hippocampal region (Teicher, 2002). There is good reason to suppose that brain growth is hampered in children who are repeatedly traumatised. A major mechanism is the damage done by constantly having cortisol secreted, the fight-flight hormone (Tarullo & Gunnar, 2006).

27 **such as the hormone dopamine:** A child who has been persistently deprived of pleasure is likely, in later life, to be more impulsive and to be attracted to short-term rewards, like substance abuse (drugs and alcohol) or quick-fix pleasure hits (like casual sex) (Read et al., 2014). All this shows up in the biology both of maltreated children and of the distressed adults they become. It changes their brains and brainwave patterns.

27 **a greater likelihood of schizophrenia:** Fosse et al., 2015.

27 **for attention deficit hyperactivity disorder:** Ruttle et al., 2014.

28 **psychosis and childhood maltreatment:** E.g. Ajnakina et al., 2016; Daruy-Filho et al., 2011.

Chapter 3

31 **prone to explosive irritability and defensiveness:** Matějček et al., 1978, 1980.

31 **to be emotionally insecure aged 30–40:** Broussard & Cassidy, 2010.

31 **for the child when it grew up:** Herman et al., 2006; Myhrman et al., 1996.

31 **having been unwanted makes this much more likely:** McNeil et al., 2009.

33 **of suicide in high academic achievers:** Aläräisanen et al., 2006.

33 **of having to people-please parents:** Miller, 1997b.

34 **dislike me or have it in for me:** NSPCC, 2001.

34 **hostility towards their step-children:** Lawson & Mace, 2009.

Notes

34   **whether at school or at home:** Arseneault et al., 2011; Schreier et al., 2009; Read & Argyle, 2005.

36   **risk factors for schizophrenia:** Read & Dillon, 2013, chap. 18.

36   **put at two to three times greater risk:** Morgan et al., 2007.

37   **as was the case with Terry:** Rubino et al., 2009.

41   **the likelihood of a further episode:** Hooley, 2007.

41   **likewise Peggy's irascibility (and Margaret's):** Goldstein, 1985; Schiffman et al., 2002; Wahlberg et al., 1997.

42   **the greater the risk of schizophrenia:** Pederson et al., 2001.

42   **to hear voices and fear persecution:** Ellett et al., 2008.

42   **to suffer from schizophrenia:** Bentall, 2004.

42   **the poorer you were, the greater your risk:** Gottesman, 1992.

42   **children of West Indian immigrants to Britain:** Fearon & Morgan, 2006.

43   **this minority cause the increased rate:** Hutchinson et al., 1996; McKenzie & Murray, 1999.

43   **than those living in non-white areas:** Boydell et al., 2001.

43   **from their mothers and half from their fathers:** Bhugra et al., 1997.

43   **to have any recurrence of the illness:** Susser & Wanderling, 1994.

45   **15% of schizophrenics eventually commit suicide:** Bentall, 2004.

45   **a sense of disorientated emptiness:** Bentall, 2004.

Chapter 4

54   **have been emotionally neglected or maltreated:** Dozier et al., 2010.

55   **their babies when they are 1 year old:** Hobson et al., 2009.

55   **it will become and its brain chemistry:** The following discussion on mothering in animals is based on O'Connor & Cameron, 2006.

57   **goes for monkeys seems to go for humans:** James, 2016, chap. 6; Read & Bentall, 2012; Sroufe et al., 2009.

57   **the crucial role of early nurture:** Jaffee, 2007.

57   **their own children or provided inadequate care:** Sroufe et al., 2009.

58   **and that man hands on emotional health, as well:** James, 2016.

58   **such as having had love from another relative:** Sroufe et al., 2009.

59   **maddening and, especially, depressing to children:** Barber et al., 2005.

59   **over-control on the part of the Italians:** Raudino et al., 2013.

62   **institutionalised children who have been fostered:** Rutter et al., 2010.

64   **febrile moods and a feeling of unreality:** Bradley & Westen, 2005.

64   **disrupted parenting before the age of 2:** Quinton & Rutter, 1988.

64   **sample of infants through to the age of 18:** Ogawa et al., 1997.

64   **from birth through to age 19:** Dutra et al., 2009.

65 **throughout her offspring's childhood:** Feldman, 2010.
65 **unresponsive early care to adult schizoid-spectrum disorders:** Lahti et al., 2009.
65 **are common in the personality-disordered:** Bradley & Westen, 2005.
66 **about two thirds of personality-disordered adults:** Bradley et al., 2005.
66 **witnessing the maltreatment of his brother:** Sar et al., 2006.
66 **a predictor of personality disorder:** Parker et al., 1999.
66 **more severe the maltreatment, the worse the outcome:** Kim et al., 2009.
67 **on their children to succeed and be perfectionists:** Thompson et al., 2000.
68 **(fantasies of being able to achieve anything) defences:** Morf & Rhode-walt, 2001.
68 **common in people with personality disorder:** Bradley & Westen, 2005.
68 **is strongly associated with personality disorder:** Ross & Krukowski, 2003.
68 **are also linked to success, especially in teenagers:** Aalsma et al., 2006; James, 2012.
69 **the latter causing the former, in most cases:** Trull et al., 2000.
69 **compulsive sexual behaviour also go together:** Raymond et al., 2003.
69 **a strong indication of personality disorder:** Dozier et al., 2010; Sar et al., 2006.

Chapter 5

72 **they can also recognise when others do so:** The following examples of pretence are based on Friedman & Leslie, 2007.
78 **than did those in other countries:** Singer et al., 2009.
78 **child, parent or other family member:** Lillard et al. 2010.
79 **show that these are numerous:** Singer et al., 2009.
80 **become sad and angry, or just withdrawn:** Bowlby, 1969, 1973.
80 **convincing evidence that this can cause distress:** James, 2010, Review 3. In particular, small children in group child care play less than do those cared for by a single carer, because so much group care is of insufficient quality. There is frequent turnover of carers, too high a ratio of carers to children and insufficient individual attention. Such low-quality care can cause aimless, 'lost' behaviour in toddlers. Solitary play and aimless wandering are common in children in low-quality group care (Vandell & Powers, 1983). Where quality is higher, children play more competently with substitute carers, peers and objects (Howes & Stewart, 1987). The extent of creative play activity is a significant predictor of their mental capacities in group-cared toddlers (Howes & Smith, 1996).

Notes

80 **reflects how they have been cared for:** Distress-filled narratives found at age 5 predict levels of emotional distress measured in the child a year later (Warren et al., 2000): measured at age 5, negative expectations of others in narratives significantly predict parental and teacher reports of internalising (self-attacking, withdrawn) and anxiety (irrational fears) symptoms in the 6-year-old. Child negative expectations caused by their nurture predict later anxiety much better than do levels of actual parental anxiety and measures of child temperament. Nonetheless, when all the studies are reviewed, there is a close link between the content of the irrational fears of parents and those of children (Hadwin et al., 2006). This shows the extent to which the concerns of the parents become those of the child. These parental issues come to be expressed in children's imaginary stories.

Specific kinds of narratives have been linked to specific kinds of maltreatment. The physically abused are most likely to engage in role-reversal in stories, becoming the carer, repairing damaged parents (Macfie et al., 1999). This is a simple way for such children to cope with the feeling of being damaged themselves. They invent stories in which they look after the parent and, in doing so, have a feeling of looking after themselves, by identifying with the imaginary parent. They are also seeking to heal the distress the parent (with whom they are identified) suffers.

Both physically abused and neglected children often represent the self in stories as angry and oppositional towards others. Neglected children also represent others as hurt, sad or anxious more frequently than do both abused and non-maltreated children. Compared with all other children, sexually abused children represent others as liking them and, compared with physically abused children, more often express the wish to be close to others (Waldinger et al., 2001). This suggests that sexual abuse creates cravings for admiration and love.

80 **lack of impulse control when with other children:** Warren et al., 1996.

80 **more dissociation than those of the non-maltreated:** Macfie et al., 2001.

81 **with divorced parents reveal similar dissociation:** Page & Bretherton, 2001.

82 **as children relate directly to its content:** Bowe, 2002; Falukozi & Addington, 2012; Hardy et al., 2005; Read et al., 1999; Reiff et al., 2012.

82 **maltreatment leads to specific adult difficulties:** E.g. Keyes et al., 2012; Longden et al., 2015.

82 **city centre violent crime is 'What are you looking at?:** James, 1995.

82 **or with other coercive, negative care:** James, 1995; Lansford et al., 2002; Maxfield & Widom, 1996.

82 **as a result of a lack of early care:** Pickering et al., 2008.

82 **because of gender or race):** Janssen et al., 2003.

82   rendered powerless by early care or subsequent experience: Mirowsky & Ross, 1983.

83   are more likely to experience dissociation: Varese et al., 2012.

85   in those who have been sexually abused: Varese et al., 2012.

85   different kinds of childhood experience predict them: Bentall et al., 2012.

86   Sure enough, as found in nine other studies: Shevlin et al., 2008.

86   as parents without a schizophrenic offspring (65%, vs 35%): Karon & Widener, 1994.

87   a basic fault line in identity development: Bradley & Westen, 2005; Lanius et al., 2010.

87   and they pass down the generations: James, 2016, chap. 6.

89   from ones not induced by drugs: Mitchell & Vierkand, 1991.

Chapter 6

94   entailed authenticity on stage, not acting: Ladkin, 2010.

95   deep feelings dating back to childhood: Ladkin, 2010.

97   *Hollywood Babylon*: Anger, 1975.

102   giving grounds for that confidence: Bellis et al., 2012.

102   the creative are more psychotic: Ando et al., 2014; Jamison, 2011; Kyaga et al., 2011.

102   could be traced to adverse childhood experiences: The discussion on ACEs in the following paragraphs is summarised from Bellis et al., 2012.

103   more common on the part of both fame-seekers: North et al., 2007.

103   and the famous: Young & Pinsky 2006.

103   insightfulness he was showing in 'Rock 'N' Roll Suicide': The discussion on suicide in this and the next paragraph are summarised from Hecht, 2014, p. 149 onwards.

108   all too visible in a film taken of the visit: See the end of the *Andy Warhol – At The Factory* video (www.dailymotion.com/video/x7ixb6_andy-warhol-at-the-factory-david-bo_creation).

Chapter 7

112   simply up sticks and move to another location: Sahlins, 2003.

112   like a pirate among his "tough" young friends': W. James, 1890.

112   key studies by Susan Harter and colleagues: Harter et al., 1997.

114   they are primarily false in that relationship: Harter et al., 1997.

117   see their positive attributes as these components: Miller, 1997a.

118   all the other glories of pretend play: Wyman et al., 2009.

Notes

119   **upon whom I draw extensively in what follows:** Humphrey & Dennett, 1989.

124   **widely accepted that MPD is a real phenomenon:** Gillig, 2009; Ross, 2006; Sar et al., 2006.

124   **a woman who underwent psychotherapy for 15 years:** Waldfogel et al., 2007.

125   **a new Bianchi emerged, called Steve:** A video of this transformation is available at: www.youtube.com/watch?v=Ibj-b3OlrgQ

126   **comes from Shaun Nichols and Stephen Stich:** Nichols & Stich, 2000.

128   **a little-read essay by Stanley James:** S. James, 2004.

Chapter 8

143   **my book *How to Develop Emotional Health*:** James, 2014a.

144   **were asked about their sexual preferences:** Ariely & Loewenstein, 2005.

145   **having been shown to strongly influence them:** James, 2016.

145   **our traits vary considerably, depending on context:** Sheldon et al., 1997.

146   **all contexts, but, rather, as feeling authentic:** Sheldon et al., 1997.

147   **student, employee, child, friend and romantic partner:** Sheldon et al., 1997.

148   **This derives from our childhood history:** James, 2016.

Chapter 9

149   **a TV programme available on the Internet:** The programme was called 'The Man Who Shot John Lennon', first broadcast in the UK in 1988 and subsequently in the US (https://www.youtube.com/watch?v=kFa4wuY1zgk).

153   **have demonstrated this for placebo pills:** Benedetti, 2014; Healy, 1999; Kirsch, 2009.

153   **based on the belief that they will work:** E.g. Pigott et al., 2010.

154   **to enhance performance is an effective strategy:** Watson, 2011 ; Watson & Czech, 2005; Watson & Nesti, 2005.

154   **never any doubt that you would nail it':** Syed, 2010, pp. 165–166.

156   **ego state therapy:** Emerson, 2007.

156   **parts therapy:** Hunter, 2005.

156   **Eric Berne's concept:** Berne, 1961.

160   **still affecting its victims 60 years later:** Rusby & Tasker, 2008, 2009.

161   **a sensible decision by Adult Olga:** Birger, 2015.

161   **described so well by Eleanor Longden:** E.g. Longden et al., 2012.

REFERENCES

Aalsma, M.C., et al. (2006). Personal fables, narcissism and adolescent adjustment. *Psychology in the Schools, 43*: 481–491.

Ajnakina, O., et al. (2016). Impact of childhood adversities on specific symptom dimensions in first-episode psychosis. *Psychological Medicine, 46* (2), 317–326.

Aläräisanen, A., et al. (2006). Good school performance is a risk factor of suicide in psychoses: A 35-year follow-up of the Northern Finland 1966 Birth Cohort. *Acta Psychiatrica Scandinavica, 114*: 357–362.

Alexander, P.C., et al. (1998). Adult attachment and long-term effects in survivors of incest. *Child Abuse and Neglect, 22*: 45–61.

Ando, V., et al. (2014). Psychotic traits in comedians. *British Journal of Psychiatry, 204* (5): 341–345.

Anger, K. (1975). *Hollywood Babylon*. New York: Dell.

APA (2013). *Diagnostic and Statistical Manual of Mental Disorders, Fifth Edition (DSM–5)*. Washington, DC: American Psychiatric Association.

Ariely, D., & Loewenstein, G. (2005). The heat of the moment: The effect of sexual arousal on sexual decision making. *Journal of Behavioural Decision Making, 19*: 87–98.

Arseneault, L., et al. (2011). Childhood trauma and children's emerging psychotic symptoms: A genetically sensitive longitudinal cohort study. *American Journal of Psychiatry, 168*: 65–72.

Barber, B.K., et al. (2005). Parental support, psychological control and behavioural control: Assessing relevance across time, culture and method. *Monographs of the Society for Research in Child Development, 70*, 1–151.

References

Bellis, M.A., et al. (2012). Dying to be famous: Retrospective cohort of rock and pop star mortality and its association with adverse childhood experiences. *BMJ Open, 2* (6), available at: http://bmjopen.bmj.com/content/2/6/e002089.full

Benedetti, F. (2014). *Placebo Effects: Understanding the Mechanisms in Health and Disease.* Oxford: Oxford University Press.

Bentall, R.P. (2004). *Madness Explained.* London: Penguin.

Bentall, R.P., et al. (2012). Do specific early-life adversities lead to specific symptoms of psychosis? A study from the 2007 The Adult Psychiatric Morbidity Survey. *Schizophrenia Bulletin, 38*: 534–540.

Berne, E. (1961). *Transactional Analysis in Psychotherapy.* New York: Grove Press.

Bhugra, D., et al. (1997). Incidence and outcome of schizophrenia in Whites, African-Caribbeans and Asians in London. *Psychological Medicine, 27*: 791–798.

Birger, J. (2015). *Date-onomics – How Dating Became a Lop-sided Numbers Game.* New York: Workman Publishing.

Bowe, S. (2002). *The Relationship Between Childhood Trauma and Auditory Hallucinations.* Doctoral Dissertation, University of Leeds, Leeds.

Bowlby, J. (1969). *Attachment, Vol. 1. Attachment and Loss.* London: Penguin.

Bowlby, J. (1973). *Attachment, Vol. 2. Attachment and Loss: Separation: Anxiety and Anger.* London: Penguin.

Boydell, J., et al. (2001). Incidence of schizophrenia in ethnic minorities in London. *British Medical Journal, 323*: 1–4.

Bradley, R., & Westen, D. (2005). The psychodynamics of borderline personality disorder: A view of developmental psychopathology. *Development and Psychopathology, 17*: 927–957.

Bradley, R., et al. (2005). Etiology of borderline personality disorder. *Journal of Nervous and Mental Disease, 193*: 24–31.

Broussard, E.R., & Cassidy, J. (2010). Maternal perception of newborns predicts attachment organization in middle adulthood. *Attachment & Human Development, 12*: 159–172.

Cannon, M., et al. (2003). Prenatal and perinatal risk factors for schizophrenia. In: R. Murray et al. (Eds.), *The Epidemiology of Schizophrenia.* Cambridge: Cambridge University Press.

References

Daruy-Filho, L., et al. (2011). Childhood maltreatment and clinical outcomes of bipolar disorder. *Acta Psychiatrica Scandinavica, 124,* 427–434.

Di Forti, M., et al. (2009). High-potency cannabis and the risk of psychosis. *British Journal of Psychiatry, 195* (6): 488–491.

Dozier, M., et al. (2010). Attachment and psychopathology in adulthood. In: J. Cassidy & P.R. Shaver (Eds.), *Handbook of Attachment.* New York: Guilford.

Dutra, L., et al. (2009). Quality of early care and childhood trauma: A prospective study of developmental pathways to dissociation. *Journal of Nervous and Mental Disease, 197*: 383–390.

Ellett, L., et al. (2008). The psychological effect of an urban environment on individuals with persecutory delusions. *Schizophrenia Research, 99*: 77–84.

Emerson, G. (2007). *Ego State Therapy.* Bancyfelin: Crown House Publishing.

Falukozi, E., & Addington, J. (2012). Impact of trauma on attenuated psychotic symptoms. *Psychosis, 4*: 203–212.

Fearon, P., & Morgan, C. (2006). Environmental factors in schizophrenia. *Schizophrenia Bulletin, 32*: 405–408.

Feldman, R. (2010). The relational basis of adolescent adjustment: Trajectories of mother–child interactive behaviours from infancy to adolescence shape adolescents' adaptation. *Attachment and Human Development, 12*: 173–192.

Fisher, H.L., et al. (2011). Reliability and comparability of psychosis patients' retrospective reports of childhood abuse. *Schizophrenia Bulletin, 37*, 546–553.

Fosse, R., et al. (2015). Schizophrenia: A critical view on genetic effects. *Psychosis, 8*: 72–84.

Friedman, O., & Leslie, A.M. (2007). The conceptual underpinnings of pretence: Pretending is not 'behaving-as-if'. *Cognition, 105*: 103–124.

Gillig, P.M. (2009). Dissociative identity disorder: A controversial diagnosis. *Psychiatry (Edgmont), 6*: 24–29.

Gillman, P., & Gillman, L. (1987). *Alias David Bowie.* Los Angeles, CA: New English Library.

References

Goldstein, M.J. (1985). Family factors that antedate the onset of schizophrenia and related disorders. *Acta Psychiatrica Scandinavica, 319*: 7–18.

Gottesman, I.I. (1992). *Schizophrenia Genesis*. New York: Freeman.

Hadwin, J.A., et al. (2006). The development of information processing biases in childhood anxiety: A review and exploration of its origins in parenting. *Clinical Psychology Review, 26* (7): 876–894.

Hardy, A., et al. (2005). Trauma and hallucinatory experience in psychosis. *Journal of Nervous and Mental Disease, 193*: 501–507.

Harter, S., et al. (1997). The development of multiple role-related selves during adolescence. *Development and Psychopathology, 9*: 835–853.

Healy, D. (1999). *The Antidepressant Era*. Boston, MA: Harvard University Press.

Hecht, J. (2014). *Stay – A History of Suicide and the Philosophies Against It*. New Haven, CT: Yale University Press.

Herman, D.B., et al. (2006). Does unwantedness of pregnancy predict schizophrenia in the offspring?' *Social Psychiatry and Psychiatric Epidemiology, 41*: 605–610.

Hobson, R.P., et al. (2009). How mothers with borderline personality disorder relate to their year-old infants. *British Journal of Psychiatry, 195* (4): 325–330.

Hooley, J.M. (2007). Expressed emotion and relapse of psychopathology. *Annual Review of Clinical Psychology, 3*: 329–352.

Howes, C., & Stewart, P. (1987). Child's play with adults, toys, and peers: An examination of family and child-care influences. *Developmental Psychology, 23* (3): 423–430.

Howes, C., & Smith, E.W. (1996). Relations among child care quality, teacher behaviour, children's play activities, emotional security and cognitive activity in child care. *Early Childhood Research Quarterly, 10* (4): 381–404.

Humphrey, N., & Dennet, D.C. (1989). Speaking for ourselves. In: D.C. Dennet, *Brainchildren: Essays on Designing Minds*. Cambridge, MA: Bradford Books, MIT Press, 1999.

Hunter, C.R. (2005). *Hypnosis for Inner Conflict Resolution: Introducing Parts Therapy*. Bancyfelin: Crown House Publishing.

Hutchinson, G., et al. (1996). Morbid risk of schizophrenia in first-degree relatives of white and African-Caribbean patients with psychosis. *British Journal of Psychiatry, 169* (6): 776–780.

Jaffee, S.R. (2007). Sensitive, stimulating caregiving predicts cognitive and behavioral resilience in neuro-developmentally at-risk infants. *Development and Psychopathology, 19*: 631–647.

James, O.W. (1995). *Juvenile Violence in a Winner–Loser Culture*. London: Free Association Books.

James, O.W. (2010). *How Not To F*** Them Up*. London: Vermilion.

James, O.W. (2012). *Office Politics – How to Thrive in a World of Lying, Backstabbing and Dirty Tricks*. London: Vermilion.

James, O.W. (2014a). *How to Develop Emotional Health*. London: Macmillan.

James, O.W. (2014b). Not in your genes – time to accept the null hypothesis of the Human Genome Project?' *ATTACHMENT: New Directions in Psychotherapy and Relational Psychoanalysis, 8*: 281–296.

James, O.W. (2016). *Not In Your Genes – The Real Reasons Why Children Are Like Their Parents*. London: Vermilion.

James, S. (2004). *Pretenses and Selves*. Available at: http://wanderingstan.com/files/Pretense_and_Selves.pdf

James, W. (1890). *The Principles of Psychology*. New York: Henry Holt and Company.

Jamison, K.J. (2011). Great wits and madness: More near allied?' *British Journal of Psychiatry, 199* (5): 351–352.

Janssen, I., et al. (2003). Discrimination and delusional ideation. *British Journal of Psychiatry, 182* (1): 71–76.

Karon, B., & Widener, A.J. (1994). Is there really a schizophregenic parent?' *Psychoanalytic Psychology, 11*: 47–61.

Keyes, K.M., et al. (2012). Childhood maltreatment and the structure of common psychiatric disorders. *British Journal of Psychiatry, 200* (2): 107–115.

Khan, M.M. (1963). The concept of cumulative trauma. *Psychoanalytic Study of the Child, 18*: 286–306.

Kim, J., et al. (2009). Child maltreatment and trajectories of personality and behavioural functioning: Implications for the development of personality disorder. *Development and Psychopathology, 21*: 889–912.

References

Kirsch, I. (2009). *The Emperor's New Drugs: Exploding the Antidepressant Myth*. Oxford: Bodley Head.

Klerman, G.L. (1978). The evolution of a scientific nosology. In: J.C. Shershow (Ed.), *Schizophrenia: Science and Practice* (pp. 99–121). Cambridge, MA: Harvard University Press.

Kohut, H. (1978). The disorders of the self and their treatment. *International Journal of Psychoanalysis, 59*: 413–425.

Konings, M., et al. (2012). Replication in two independent population-based samples that childhood maltreatment and cannabis use synergistically impact on psychosis risk. *Psychological Medicine, 42*: 149–159.

Kraepelin, E. (2012). *Lectures on Clinical Psychiatry*. Charleston, SC: Nabu Press.

Kyaga, S., et al. (2011). Creativity and mental disorder: Family study of 300,000 people with severe mental disorder. *British Journal of Psychiatry, 199* (5): 373–379.

Ladkin, D. (2010). Enacting the 'true self': Towards a theory of embodied authentic leadership. *The Leadership Quarterly, 21*: 64–74.

Lahti, J., et al. (2009). Early-life origins of schizotypal traits in adulthood. *British Journal of Psychiatry, 195* (2): 132–137.

Laing, R.D. (1960). *The Divided Self: An Existential Study in Sanity and Madness*. London: Tavistock Publications.

Laing, R.D., & Esterson, A. (1970). *Sanity, Madness and the Family*. London: Penguin.

Lanius, R.A., et al. (2010). *The Impact of Early Life Trauma on Health and Disease*. Cambridge: Cambridge University Press.

Lansford, J.E., et al. (2002). A 12-year prospective study of the long-term effects of early child physical maltreatment on psychological, behavioral and academic problems in adolescents. *Archives of Pediatric and Adolescent Medicine, 156*: 824–830.

Lawson, D.W., & Mace, R (2009). Trade-offs in modern parenting: A longitudinal study of sibling competition for parental care. *Evolution and Human Behavior, 30* (3), 170–183.

Lillard, A., et al. (2010). Pretend play and cognitive development. In: U. Goswami (Ed.) *The Wiley–Blackwell Handbook of Childhood Cognitive Development* (2nd edition), Chichester: Wiley.

References

Longden, E., et al. (2012). Dissociation, trauma and the role of lived experience: Towards a new conceptualization of voice hearing. *Psychological Bulletin, 138*: 28–76.

Longden, E., et al. (2015). Childhood adversity and psychosis: Generalised or specific effects?' *Epidemiology and Psychiatric Sciences* (July): 1–11.

Macfie, J., et al. (1999). Effect of maltreatment on preschoolers' narrative representations of responses to relieve distress and of role reversal. *Developmental Psychology, 35* (2), 460–465.

Macfie, J., et al. (2001). The development of dissociation in maltreated preschool-aged children. *Development and Psychopathology, 13* (2): 233–254.

Matějček, Z., et al. (1978). Children from unwanted pregnancies. *Acta Psychiatrica Scandinavica, 57*: 67–90.

Matějček, Z., et al. (1980). Follow-up study of children born from unwanted pregnancies. *International Journal of Behavioural Development, 3*: 243–251.

Matheson, S.L., et al. (2012). Childhood adversity in schizophrenia: A systematic meta-analysis. *Psychological Medicine, 43*: 225–235.

Maxfield, M.G., & Widom, C. (1996). The cycle of violence. *Archives of Pediatric and Adolescent Medicine, 150*: 390–395.

McKenzie, K., & Murray, R.H. (1999). Risk factors for psychosis in the UK African-Caribbean population. In: D. Bhugra & V. Bahl (Eds.), *Ethnicity: An Agenda for Mental Health*. London: Gaskell.

McNeil, T.F., et al. (2009). Unwanted pregnancy as a risk factor for offspring schizophrenia-spectrum and affective disorders in adulthood: A prospective high-risk study. *Psychological Medicine, 39*: 957–965.

Miller, A. (1997a). *Banished Knowledge: Facing Childhood Injuries*. London: Virago.

Miller, A. (1997b). *The Drama of Being a Gifted Child: The Search for a True Self*. New York: Basic Books.

Mirowsky, J., & Ross, C.E. (1983). Paranoia and the structure of powerlessness. *American Sociological Review, 48*: 228–239.

Mitchell, J., & Vierkand, A.D (1991). Delusions and hallucinations of cocaine abusers and paranoid schizophrenics: A comparative study. *Journal of Psychology: Interdisciplinary and Applied, 125*: 301–310.

References

Morf, C.C., & Rhodewalt, F. (2001). Unravelling the paradoxes of narcissism. *Psychological Inquiry, 12*: 177–196.

Morgan, C., et al. (2007). Parental separation, loss and psychosis in different ethnic groups. *Psychological Medicine, 37*: 495–503.

Mortenson, P.B., et al. (1999). Effects of family history and place and season of birth on the risk of schizophrenia. *New England Journal of Medicine, 340*: 603–608.

Myhrman, A., et al. (1996). 'Unwantedness of pregnancy and schizophrenia in the child. *British Journal of Psychiatry, 169* (5): 637–640.

Nichols, S., & Stich, S. (2000). A cognitive theory of pretence. *Cognition, 74*: 115–147.

North, A.C., et al. (2007). Attributional style, self-esteem, and celebrity worship. *Media Psychology, 9*: 291–308.

NSPCC (2001). *Child Maltreatment in the United Kingdom.* London.

O'Connor, T.G., & Cameron, J.L. (2006). Translating research findings on early experience to prevention: Animal and human evidence on early attachment relationships. *American Journal of Preventive Medicine, 31*: 175–181.

Ogawa, J., et al. (1997). Development and the fragmented self: Longitudinal study of dissociative symptomatology in a nonclinical sample. *Development and Psychopathology, 9*: 855–879.

Page, T., & Bretherton, I. (2001). Mother– and father–child attachment themes in the story completions of pre-schoolers from post-divorce families: Do they predict relationships with peers and teachers?' *Attachment and Human Development, 3*: 1–29.

Parker, G., et al. (1999). An exploration of links between early parenting experiences and personality disorder type and disordered personality functioning. *Journal of Personality Disorders, 13*: 361–374.

Pederson, C.B., et al. (2001). Evidence of a dose–response relationship between urbanicity during upbringing and schizophrenia risk. *Archives of General Psychiatry, 58* (11): 1039–1046.

Pickering, L., et al. (2008). Insecure attachment predicts proneness to paranoia but not hallucinations. *Personality and Individual Differences, 44*: 1212–1224.

Pigott, H., et al. (2010). Efficacy and effectiveness of antidepressants: current status of research. *Psychotherapy and Psychosomatics, 79*: 267–279.

References

Plomin, R., & Simpson, M.A. (2013). The future of genomics for developmentalists. *Development and Psychopathology*, *25*: 1263–1278.

Quinton, D., & Rutter, M. (1988). *Parenting Breakdown*, Aldershot: Avebury.

Raudino, A., et al. (2013). Child anxiety and parenting in England and Italy: The moderating role of maternal warmth. *Journal of Child Psychology and Psychiatry*, *54*: 1318–1326.

Raymond, N.C., et al. (2003). Psychiatric comorbidity and compulsive/impulsive traits in compulsive sexual behaviour. *Comprehensive Psychiatry*, *44*: 370–380.

Read, J., & Argyle, N. (2005). Childhood trauma, psychosis and schizophrenia: A literature review and clinical implications. *Acta Psychiatrica Scandinavica*, *112*: 330–350.

Read, J., & Bentall, R.P. (2012). Negative childhood experiences and mental health. *British Journal of Psychiatry*, *200* (2): 89–91.

Read, J., & Dillon, J. (2013). *Models of Madness* (2nd edition). London: Routledge.

Read, J., & Gumley, B. (2008). Can attachment theory help explain the relationship between childhood adversity and psychosis?' *Attachment*, *2*: 1–35

Read, J., et al. (1999). Hallucinations, delusions and thought disorder among adult psychiatric patients with a history of child abuse. *Psychiatric Services*, *50*: 1467–1472.

Read, J., et al. (2008). Childhood maltreatment and psychosis. *Clinical Schizophrenia and Related Psychoses*, *2*: 235–254.

Read, J., et al. (2014). The traumagenic neurodevelopmental model of psychosis revisited. *Neuropsychiatry*, *4*: 65–79.

Reiff, M., et al. (2012). Childhood abuse and the content of adult psychiatric symptoms. *Psychological Trauma: Theory, Research, Practice and Policy*, *4*: 356–359.

Ross, C.A. (2006). Dissociative identity disorder. *Current Psychosis and Therapeutic Reports*, *4*: 112–116.

Ross, S.R., & Krukowski, R.A. (2003). The impostor phenomenon and maladaptive personality. *Personality and Individual Differences*, *34*: 477–484.

Rubino, A., et al. (2009). Early adverse experiences in schizophrenia

References

and unipolar depression. *Journal of Nervous and Mental Disease, 197*: 65–68.

Rusby, J.S.M., & Tasker, F. (2008). Childhood temporary separation: Long-term effects of the British evacuation of children during World War 2 on older adults' attachment styles. *Attachment and Human Development, 10*: 207–221.

Rusby, J.S.M.,& Tasker, F. (2009). Long-term effects of the British evacuation of children during World War 2 on their adult mental health. *Aging and Mental Health, 13*: 391–404.

Rutter, M., et al. (2010). *Deprivation-specific Psychological Patterns: Effects of Institutional Deprivation* (Monographs of the Society for Research in Child Development, Vol. 75, No. 1). London: Wiley.

Ruttle, P.L., et al. (2014). Adolescent internalizing symptoms and negative life events: The sensitizing effect of earlier life stress and cortisol. *Development and Psychopathology, 26*: 1411–1422.

Sahlins, M. (2003). *Stone Age Economics*. London: Routledge.

Sar, V., et al. (2006). Axis I Dissociative disorder comorbidity in borderline personality disorder and reports of childhood trauma. *Journal of Clinical Psychiatry, 67*: 1583–1590.

Schiffman, J., et al. (2002). Perception of parent–child relationships in high-risk families and adult schizophrenia outcome of offspring. *Journal of Psychiatric Research, 36*: 41–47.

Schreier A., et al. (2009). Prospective study of peer victimization in childhood and psychotic symptoms in a nonclinical population at age 12 years. *Archives of General Psychiatry, 66*: 527–536.

Sheldon, K.M., et al. (1997). Trait self and true self: Cross-role variation in the big-five personality traits and its relations with psychological authenticity and subjective well-being. *Journal of Personality and Social Psychology, 73*: 1380–1393.

Shevlin, M., et al. (2008). Cumulative trauma and psychosis: An analysis of the National Comorbidity Survey and the British Psychiatric Morbidity Survey. *Schizophrenia Bulletin, 34*: 193–199.

Singer, D.G., et al. (2009). Children's pastimes and play in sixteen nations: Is free play declining?' *American Journal of Play, 1*: 283–312.

Snellen, M., et al. (1999). Schizophrenia, mental state and mother–infant

References

interaction: Examining the relationship. *Australian and New Zealand Journal of Psychology, 33*: 902–911.

Sroufe, L.A., et al. (2009). *The Development of the Person: The Minnesota Study of Risk and Adaptation from Birth to Adulthood.* New York: Guilford Press.

Susser, E., & Wanderling, J. (1994). Epidemiology of nonaffective acute remitting psychoses vs. schizophrenia: Sex and sociocultural setting. *Archives of General Psychiatry, 51*: 294–301.

Syed, M. (2010). *Bounce – The Myth of Talent and the Power of Practice.* London: Fourth Estate.

Tarullo, A.R., & Gunnar, M.R. (2006). Child maltreatment and the development of the HPA axis. *Hormones and Behaviour, 50*: 632–639.

Teicher, M.H. (2002). Scars that won't heal: The neurobiology of child abuse. *Scientific American, 286*: 54–61.

Thompson, T., et al. (2000). Impostor fears and perfectionist concern over mistakes. *Personality and Individual Differences, 29*: 629–647.

Trull, T.J., et al. (2000). Borderline personality disorder and substance use disorders: A review and integrations. *Clinical Psychology Review, 20*: 235–253.

Vandell, D.L., & Powers, C.P. (1983). Day care quality and children's free play activities. *American Journal of Orthopsychiatry, 53* (3): 493–500.

Varese, F., et al. (2012). Childhood adversities increase the risk of psychosis: A meta-analysis of patient-control, prospective and cross-sectional cohort studies. *Schizophrenia Bulletin, 36*: 661–671.

Wahlberg, K.E., et al. (1997). Gene–environment interaction in vulnerability to schizophrenia. *American Journal of Psychiatry, 154*: 355–362.

Waldfogel, B., et al. (2007). Sighted and blind in one person: A case report and conclusions on the psychoneurobiology of vision. *Nervenarzt, 78*: 1303–1309.

Waldinger, R.J., et al. (2001). Maltreatment and internal representations of relationships: Core relationship themes in the narratives of abused and neglected preschoolers. *Social Development, 10*: 41–58.

Warren, S.L., et al. (1996). Can emotions and themes in children's play predict behavior problems?' *Journal of the American Academy of Child & Adolescent Psychiatry, 35*: 1331–1337.

References

Warren, S.L., et al. (2000). Internal representations: Predicting anxiety from children's play narratives. *Journal of the American Academy of Child & Adolescent Psychiatry, 39*: 100–107.

Watson, N.J. (2011). Identity in sport: A psychological and theological analysis. In: J. Parry et al. (Eds.), *Theology, Ethics and Transcendence in Sports* (pp. 107–148). London: Routledge.

Watson, N.J., & Czech, D.R. (2005). The use of prayer in sport: Implication for sport psychology counselling. *Athletic Insight, 7*: 26–35.

Watson, N.J., & Nesti, M. (2005). The role of spirituality in sport psychology consulting: An analysis and integrative review of literature. *Journal of Applied Sport Psychology, 17*: 228–239.

Wigman, J.T., et al. (2012). Early trauma and familial risk in the development of the extended psychosis phenotype in adolescence. *Acta Psychiatrica Scandinavica, 126*: 266–273.

Wyman, E., et al. (2009). Young children understand multiple pretend identities in their object play. *British Journal of Developmental Psychology, 27*: 385–404.

Young, S.M., & Pinsky, D. (2006). Narcissism and celebrity. *Journal of Research in Personality, 40*: 463–471.

INDEX

Index

Index